WITHDRAWN
UTSA LIBRARIES

ECONOMIC ISSUES, PROBLEMS AND PERSPECTIVES

FEDERAL TAXES AND FAMILIES: POLICIES AND ANALYSES

ECONOMIC ISSUES, PROBLEMS AND PERSPECTIVES

Additional books in this series can be found on Nova's website under the Series tab.

Additional E-books in this series can be found on Nova's website under the E-book tab.

FAMILY ISSUES IN THE 21ST CENTURY

Additional books in this series can be found on Nova's website under the Series tab.

Additional E-books in this series can be found on Nova's website under the E-book tab.

ECONOMIC ISSUES, PROBLEMS AND PERSPECTIVES

FEDERAL TAXES AND FAMILIES: POLICIES AND ANALYSES

TRACEY I. OWENS
AND
RENE O. REYNOLDS
EDITORS

Nova Science Publishers, Inc.
New York

Copyright © 2012 by Nova Science Publishers, Inc.

All rights reserved. No part of this book may be reproduced, stored in a retrieval system or transmitted in any form or by any means: electronic, electrostatic, magnetic, tape, mechanical photocopying, recording or otherwise without the written permission of the Publisher.

For permission to use material from this book please contact us:
Telephone 631-231-7269; Fax 631-231-8175
Web Site: http://www.novapublishers.com

NOTICE TO THE READER

The Publisher has taken reasonable care in the preparation of this book, but makes no expressed or implied warranty of any kind and assumes no responsibility for any errors or omissions. No liability is assumed for incidental or consequential damages in connection with or arising out of information contained in this book. The Publisher shall not be liable for any special, consequential, or exemplary damages resulting, in whole or in part, from the readers' use of, or reliance upon, this material. Any parts of this book based on government reports are so indicated and copyright is claimed for those parts to the extent applicable to compilations of such works.

Independent verification should be sought for any data, advice or recommendations contained in this book. In addition, no responsibility is assumed by the publisher for any injury and/or damage to persons or property arising from any methods, products, instructions, ideas or otherwise contained in this publication.

This publication is designed to provide accurate and authoritative information with regard to the subject matter covered herein. It is sold with the clear understanding that the Publisher is not engaged in rendering legal or any other professional services. If legal or any other expert assistance is required, the services of a competent person should be sought. FROM A DECLARATION OF PARTICIPANTS JOINTLY ADOPTED BY A COMMITTEE OF THE AMERICAN BAR ASSOCIATION AND A COMMITTEE OF PUBLISHERS.

Additional color graphics may be available in the e-book version of this book.

LIBRARY OF CONGRESS CATALOGING-IN-PUBLICATION DATA

ISBN: 978-1-61942-864-5

Published by Nova Science Publishers, Inc. † New York
Library
University of Texas
at San Antonio

CONTENTS

Preface		vii
Chapter 1	Federal Income Tax Treatment of the Family *Jane G. Gravelle*	1
Chapter 2	The Child Tax Credit: Current Law and Legislative History *Margot L. Crandall-Hollick*	35
Chapter 3	The Child Tax Credit: Economic Analysis and Policy Options *Margot L. Crandall-Hollick*	53
Chapter 4	Dependent Care: Current Tax Benefits and Legislative Issues *Christine Scott and Janemarie Mulvey*	77
Chapter 5	Tax Benefits for Families: Adoption *Christine Scott*	91
Chapter 6	Federal Estate, Gift, and Generation-Skipping Taxes: A Description of Current Law *John R. Luckey*	111
Index		127

PREFACE

This book examines the current federal income tax laws which differentiate among families by type and structure in several ways. This differentiation has changed considerably over the years and includes personal exemptions, standard deductions, rate schedules, and various other features such as child care credits, age exemptions, and earned income credits. Discussed also is the legislative history of the Child Tax Credit; dependent care tax benefits; the major provisions of the federal estate, gift, and generation-skipping transfer taxes; and tax benefits for the adoption of children through federal grants to states and through the tax code.

Chapter 1 - Recent years have been times of significant changes in the income tax treatment of the family. For lower-income families, the most important of these have been the expansion of the earned income credit (EIC) in 1990 and 1993. For middle-income families, the introduction of the child credit in 1997 and its expansion in 2001-2003, along with the expansion of rate brackets and standard deductions to address the marriage penalty, have been important features. For higher-income families, the lowering of tax rates in general and the increasing scope of the alternative minimum tax (AMT) are important changes. Chairman Rangel of the Ways and Means Committee proposed a reform proposal in the 110th Congress, H.R. 3970, that would make a number of changes affecting families differently, including repeal of the alternative minimum tax, a surcharge on high income families, and expansion of the earned income credit for families without children.[1] President Obama proposed to make the 2001-2003 middle class tax cuts permanent. Most recently, the 2001-2003 tax cuts, which were set to expire after 2010, were extended for an additional two years (P.L. 111-312).

Chapter 2 - The child tax credit was created in 1997 by the Taxpayer Relief Act of 1997 (P.L. 105-34) to help ease the financial burden that families incur when they have children. Like other tax credits, the child tax credit reduces tax liability on a dollar for dollar basis. Initially the child tax credit was a nonrefundable credit for most families. A nonrefundable tax credit can only reduce a taxpayer's tax liability to zero, while a refundable tax credit can exceed a taxpayer's tax liability, providing a cash payment primarily to low-income taxpayers who owe little or no income tax. Over the past 10 years, legislative changes have significantly changed the credit, transforming it from a nonrefundable credit available only to the middle and upper-middle class, to a partially refundable credit that more low-income families are eligible to claim.

Chapter 3 - Certain parameters of the child tax credit are scheduled to expire in 2012 providing an opportunity to evaluate the economic impact of the current credit and examine policy options for the credit after 2012. The Taxpayer Relief Act of 1997 (P.L. 105-34) created a $500-per-child nonrefundable tax credit to help ease the financial burden that families incur when they have children.[1] Since 2001, legislative changes, particularly those made by the Economic Growth and Tax Relief Reconciliation Act of 2001 (EGTRRA; P.L. 107-16) and the American Recovery and Reinvestment Act of 2009 (ARRA; P.L. 111-5), have altered the structure of this tax benefit. Specifically, the amount of the credit per child has increased and the credit has been made partially refundable, expanding the availability of the credit to some low-income families. These changes are scheduled to expire at the end of 2012, and the structure of the child tax credit will revert back to its pre-2001 form.

Chapter 4 - The demographics of the workforce has changed considerably in the past few decades, as has the nature of caregiving responsibilities. Not only has the share of women working increased considerably over the past three decades, but the overall workforce has aged. While many workers today still care for children, they are also increasingly more likely to be caring for aging parents.

To address dependent care costs for working caregivers, there are two current law tax provisions for dependent care: the dependent care tax credit (DCTC) and the exclusion from income for employer-provided dependent care assistance programs (DCAP). Some of the tax provisions for dependent care tax provisions are also expected to expire (not be in effect) after December 31, 2012. In addressing the expiration of these provisions, Congress may also consider whether to expand these tax incentives even more for working caregivers. The importance of this issue is underscored by the expansion of dependent care tax incentives in President Obama's Legislative Agenda[1] through the White House Middle Class Task Force chaired by Vice President Biden, which includes as one of its goals to improve work and family balance.

Chapter 5 - States have paramount responsibility in setting policy to govern the process of child adoption. Nonetheless, the federal government plays a significant—though indirect—role in supporting adoption through grants to states that provide both one-time and ongoing subsidies to parents of adoptive children with special needs and through tax benefits that help offset the costs of adopting a child. This report focuses primarily on the latter—the federal adoption tax credit and income tax exclusion for employer-provided adoption assistance.

Chapter 6 - This report contains an explanation of the major provisions of the federal estate, gift, and generation-skipping transfer taxes as they apply to transfers in 2011. The enactment of the Economic Growth and Tax Relief Reconciliation Act of 2001[1] phased out the estate and generation-skipping taxes over a 10-year period, leaving the gift tax as the only federal transfer tax in 2010. The year 2010 was the first since 1916 in which there was no federal estate tax. There was also a year hiatus for the generation-skipping tax. The Tax Relief, Unemployment Insurance Reauthorization, and Job Creation Act of 2010[2] temporarily (through the end of 2012) reinstated the estate and generation-skipping taxes with lower top rates and larger exemptions and reunified the estate and gift taxes.

In: Federal Taxes and Families ISBN: 978-1-61942-864-5
Editors: T. I. Owens and R. O. Reynolds ©2012 Nova Science Publishers, Inc.

Chapter 1

FEDERAL INCOME TAX TREATMENT OF THE FAMILY[*]

Jane G. Gravelle

SUMMARY

Individual income tax provisions have shifted over time, first in increasing the burden on larger families, and then in decreasing it. These shifts were caused by changing tax code features: personal exemptions, standard and itemized deductions, rates, the earned income credit, the child credit, and other standard structural aspects of the tax. Some of these features reflect changes made by the 2001 Bush tax cuts, which were recently extended for an additional two years by P.L. 111-312. The distribution of tax burden across income classes has, however, changed relatively little, although burdens at the top and bottom have decreased in recent years.

While several standards may be considered in determining equitable treatment of families over family type and size, a standard approach is based on ability to pay, so that large families with the same income as small ones pay less tax. Based on this standard, the analysis of equity across families suggests that families with children are paying lower rates of tax (or receiving larger negative tax rates) than single individuals and married couples at lower and middle incomes. However, families with

---

[*] This is an edited, reformatted and augmented version of a Congressional Research Service publication, CRS Report for Congress RL33755, from www.crs.gov, Prepared for Members and Committees of Congress ,dated December 21, 2010.

children are being taxed more heavily at higher-income levels. At the lowest income levels, the EIC provides the largest tax subsidies to families with two or three children. The smallest subsidies go to childless couples. At middle-income levels, families with many children will have the most favorable treatment, due to the effect of the child credit, which has a very large effect relative to tax liability. At higher-income levels, large families are penalized because the adjustments for children such as personal exemptions and child credits are too small or are phased out, while graduated rates cause larger families that need more income to maintain a given living standard to pay higher taxes. Tax rates are more variable at lower-income levels. At all but the lowest and very highest income levels, singles pay higher taxes than married couples.

The analysis of the marriage penalty indicates that marriage penalties have largely been eliminated for those without children throughout the middle-income range, but this change has inevitably expanded marriage bonuses. Marriage penalties remain at the high and low income levels and could also apply to those with children, where the penalty or bonus is not very well defined. But by and large, the current system is likely to encourage rather than discourage marriage and favors married couples over singles.

The analysis of equity across families suggests that increases in earned income tax credits for those without children would lead to more equal treatment based on the ability to pay approach, while full refundability of the child credit would exacerbate inequalities. At the higher end of the scale, eliminating phaseouts of provisions that differentiate across families would probably lead to more equitable treatment, and containing the effect of the alternative minimum tax is important to both reducing the high burden of taxes on families with children at upper middle-income levels as well as preventing an increasing level of marriage penalties.

This report does not include the temporary provisions enacted in the American Recovery and Reinvestment Act of 2009 (P.L. 111-5), although a brief summary is provided in the introduction.

INTRODUCTION

Recent years have been times of significant changes in the income tax treatment of the family. For lower-income families, the most important of these have been the expansion of the earned income credit (EIC) in 1990 and 1993. For middle-income families, the introduction of the child credit in 1997 and its expansion in 2001-2003, along with the expansion of rate brackets and standard deductions to address the marriage penalty, have been important features. For higher-income families, the lowering of tax rates in general and the increasing scope of the alternative minimum tax (AMT) are important changes. Chairman Rangel of the Ways and Means Committee proposed a reform proposal in the 110th Congress, H.R. 3970, that would make a number of changes affecting families differently, including repeal of the alternative minimum tax, a surcharge on high income families, and expansion of the earned income credit for families without children.[1] President Obama proposed to make the 2001-2003 middle class tax cuts permanent. Most recently, the 2001-2003 tax cuts, which were set to expire after 2010, were extended for an additional two years (P.L. 111-312).

The American Recovery and Reinvestment Act of 2009 (P.L. 111-5) contained temporary provisions that are aimed at middle-class and lower-income families. These provisions included a refundable payroll tax credit based on earnings limited to $800 for joint returns ($400 for singles) and phased out as income rises. It also includes an increase in the earned income tax credit, with a higher rate of 45% for families with two children and an increase in the phaseout level by $2,000 for joint returns, aimed at reducing the marriage penalty. It also included a provision increasing the refundability of the credit by allowing some refundability for incomes over $3,000. A jobs bill passed in the House in December (H.R. 2847) temporarily eliminates the $3,000 floor for 2010. These provisions expired after two years, although P.L. 111-312 extended the child credit refundability provision for two additional years. The analysis in this paper does not reflect these temporary provisions; however, the child care provision has its largest relative impact on low-income taxpayers.

Although an array of issues might be considered in discussing tax rules and their effects, this paper considers two questions: what is an equitable treatment of families of different sizes and what are the effects of marriage penalties and bonuses?

The first section summarizes the major features of the tax law affecting families and family choices, and how they developed over time, including the relatively recent introduction of large benefits for children at low- and moderate-income levels, a reversal of a trend in the past that tended to reduce these benefits through the erosion of the real value of the personal exemptions. It also summarizes the origin of the marriage penalty and marriage bonus.

The following two sections first discuss general equity issues, and then apply the ability-to-pay standard to examine how tax burdens vary by family size, across the income spectrum. The final section examines the marriage penalties and bonuses.

DEVELOPMENT OF CURRENT TAX TREATMENT OF THE FAMILY

Current federal income tax law differentiates among families by type and structure in several ways. This differentiation has changed considerably over the years and includes personal exemptions, standard deductions, rate schedules, and various other features such as child care credits, age exemptions, and earned income credits.

Personal Exemptions and Child Credits

Personal exemptions allow a certain amount per person to be exempt from tax. Combined with standard deductions, which vary by family type, they exclude a minimum level of income from tax. In 1986, these combined amounts were roughly set at the poverty level. Personal exemptions can also play a part in marriage bonuses when only one spouse works: a single individual cannot claim an unmarried companion as a dependent, whereas a husband can claim a wife (and vice versa).

The tax laws have always allowed some relief for family size through exemptions, although the original 1913 act allowed deductions only for the individual taxpayer ($3,000) and spouse ($1,000). These amounts were very large relative to incomes, but the initial income tax was not intended to reach a broad group of individuals. Even when dependent exemptions were allowed in 1917, they were only $200, small relative to the basic exemptions. The practice of allowing an equal exemption for each family member began in the early 1940s.

Personal exemptions were reduced in the initial years of the tax, then increased, then reduced again; they were last reduced in the early 1940s. The real value of the exemptions was also affected by inflation. For example, the personal exemption remained constant at $600 from 1948 through 1969, while its real value was heavily eroded through inflation. It was gradually increased over the next 10 years to $1,000, where it again remained constant until 1985. From 1948 through 1984, the personal exemption lost 63% of its purchasing power. In large part due to diminution of the real value of personal exemptions, the tax burden had shifted over time to fall more heavily on larger families.

In 1986, personal exemptions were increased and indexed, so that today the personal exemption has lost only about 24% of its purchasing power.[2] This shift of burden to families with children was changed dramatically by the adoption of the $500 child credits in the Taxpayer Relief Act of 1997 and by the increase in that credit to $1,000 in the Economic Growth and Recovery Act of 2001. In the cases where these credits apply (for children under 17), they caused the personal exemption plus the deduction equivalent of the credit to be 55% larger than its 1948 value with the $500 credit and 133% larger with the $1,000 credit for families in the 15% rate bracket; they are 23% and 70% larger respectively for families in the 25% bracket. The credit is not, however, indexed for inflation, and absent indexation its value will diminish. The $500 increase in the credit is to sunset in 2010 as well, although it may be extended or made permanent.

Not all taxpayers received the credit. It was phased out for higher incomes. The credit was not generally refundable and therefore families with no tax liability or insufficient liability to use the full credit would not receive the full benefit. An exception was made for families with three or more children where the credit could offset payroll tax in excess of the earned income tax credit.

When the child credit was doubled under the temporary provisions of the 2001 tax, an additional refundability provision was allowed for all families for income in excess of $10,000 (beginning at 10% and rising to 15%), indexed for inflation. The additional child credit was phased in initially, but accelerated in legislation adopted in 2003 and 2004.

The personal exemption is also phased out for higher incomes, although that phaseout is scheduled to expire.

Standard Deduction or Flat Exclusion and Itemized Deductions

Standard deductions, which vary across the types of returns (single, joint, and head of household), also affect tax burdens across families. Prior to the 2001 tax revision, the standard deductions for singles and heads of household were 60% and 80%, respectively, of the size of the deduction for joint returns. The standard deduction can contribute to a marriage penalty if it is larger than half the deduction for married couples: two singles who both work and marry will have a smaller combined deduction. It can also contribute to a marriage bonus, if there is only one earner in the couple, because the joint deduction is larger than the single deduction. In 2001, joint standard deductions were increased, so as to eliminate the marriage penalty relative to singles without children and reduce it relative to heads of household (where the deduction is 73% as large). These changes increased the marriage bonus.

Virtually from its inception, the tax law allowed deductions for taxes, interest, charitable contributions, and certain other personal expenses. In 1944, a standard deduction of 10% of adjusted gross income with a ceiling of $500 was allowed as a substitute for these itemized deductions.[3] A major reason for this exemption was to reduce the number of itemizers and make tax filing less complex. In 1964, a minimum standard deduction of $200 plus $100 for each exemption with a $1,000 ceiling was added. Beginning in 1969, these standard deductions were increased substantially. The percentage standard deduction was gradually increased to 16% and the ceiling increased to $2,000. A low-income allowance of $1,100, to be reduced by $50 in each of the next two years, was substituted for the minimum standard deduction. (These reductions were included because of the rise in the personal exemption that was increasing total exempt amounts). The low-income allowance was increased to $1,300 in 1972.

In 1975, the low-income allowance was once again differentiated, but based on family type (joint, head of household, single) rather than size. Joint returns received a $2,100 allowance by 1976. The ceiling on the percentage standard deduction was also differentiated by family type and was raised to $2,800 for joint returns by 1976. In 1977, the low-income allowance and the percentage standard deduction were consolidated into a single flat allowance called the zero-bracket amount, which was set at $3,200 in 1977 and at $3,400 in 1978. This zero-bracket amount was indexed in 1981, so that it would rise with inflation. The Tax Reform Act of 1986 raised the flat deduction amount, but continued to differentiate it with respect to family status (but not family size). The 2001 act increased the standard deduction for joint returns to twice that of single returns.

In comparing the relative benefits over time, it is important to consider the changes in all flat allowances as well, not just the personal exemption. For example, while the real value of the personal exemption has declined about 24% since 1948, the exempt amount for a family of four (joint return) was very close to the exempt amount had 1948 values been indexed for inflation (using the GDP deflator) prior to the 2001 tax changes. Current levels are about 21% larger than those that would have occurred had the exempt level in 1948 been indexed.[4] Ignoring the child credit, smaller families have more generous exempt levels today, whereas larger families have less generous levels. For example (again, ignoring the child credit), exempt allowances are larger in real terms today for singles (75% larger), for heads of households with one child or two children (46% and 20% larger, respectively) and for joint returns with one to four children (39%, 31%, 11%, and 4% larger, respectively). Real levels are about the same as 1948 for heads of household with four family members and smaller for those with more family members (1% for a five-person family, 6% for a six-person family). They are also smaller for joint-return families with five and six family members (2% and 5%, respectively).

Heads of household and joint returns with children eligible for the child credit, however, have greater exempt levels. For joint returns, assuming that additional members are eligible children, the credit causes all of them to have increased exempt amount equivalents between 87% and 117% higher than in 1948, with the larger increases for heads of households and large families with joint returns (whose values have tended to more than double).

Note, however, that changes in benefits compared with past levels do not necessarily have implications for the appropriate treatment of different families. If past family differentiation was not due to a theory about equitable treatment of differing families, there is no economic reason that current tax treatment should conform to any past standards.

Most taxpayers take the standard deduction but about a third itemize, largely at the higher-income levels. Itemized deductions tend to keep pace with income levels. They are technically subject to a phaseout but the effect of the phaseout is to increase marginal tax rates, since it is triggered by income and not deductions.

Rate Structure

Two important aspects of the rate structure are the unit of taxation and the progressivity of the rate structure (i.e., how tax rates rise as increments of income increase). Current tax rates are imposed at 10%, 15%, 25%, 28%, 33%, and 35% under the provisions of the 2001 tax change; if those provisions expire at the end of 2012, the 10% rate will return to 15% and the top four rates will increase to 28%, 31%, 36%, and 39.6%. Taxes are imposed on family units. Married couples cannot use the single rate schedules (although they can file separately with a rate structure that offers no advantage over joint filing). Most taxpayers have income that taxes them at no more than 10% (23% of returns), no more than 15% (41% of returns), and no more than 25% (15% of returns).[5]

The width of the brackets is greatest for joint returns and smallest for singles, although all types of returns reach the top 35% rate at the same point. For single returns the 10% and 15% brackets are half the width of joint returns, the 25% bracket is 70% as large, and the next two brackets are about 124% as large (longer brackets at the top being necessary to get to the same income for the top bracket). For heads of household the 10% and 15% brackets are 72% and 66% as wide, the next two about the same length and the final bracket 111% as wide.[6] There are also phaseouts of itemized deductions, personal exemptions, and child credits at very high income levels, although the itemized deduction and personal exemption phase-out has been suspended through 2012.[7] The higher rates and the phaseouts apply to only a small fraction of taxpayers. Less than 10% of taxpayers had adjusted gross income over $100,000 in 2003 and less than 2% had incomes over $200,000.[8]

In the original 1913 tax law, a single rate structure was applied to all taxpayers as individuals. In 1948, joint returns were allowed that effectively permitted income splitting. This change had little to do with any theory regarding the tax treatment of the family. Rather, it occurred because married couples in community property states were successfully claiming the right to divide their income evenly for tax purposes. Under a graduated rate structure, this income-splitting reduces the total tax burden by reducing the amount of income subject to higher rates. Income-splitting was adopted to equalize treatment across the states and to forestall a major tax-induced disruption in state property laws. This move created the familiar joint and single returns. Both the community property treatment and the legislated income-splitting resulted in a tax subsidy for marriage. Individuals who married would experience lower tax liabilities due to the rate structure as long as their incomes were unequal. Shortly after, in 1951, a head-of-household schedule for unmarried taxpayers with dependents was introduced, which allowed half the benefits from income splitting (i.e., wider tax brackets). This treatment could, in theory, create a marriage penalty for families with children, although this point received virtually no attention.

Criticism from singles, arguing that their taxes were too high, led in 1969 to a singles rate schedule with wider brackets. This difference in rate schedules, however, also created a marriage penalty for certain types of families, including those without children. If both spouses worked, tax bills could increase with marriage. Many people were uncomfortable with a tax provision that encouraged couples to live together without benefit of matrimony. Coupled with increasing female labor force participation and a changing social structure, the marriage penalty created considerable concern. For this reason, a capped deduction for the secondary earner in a family was adopted in 1981. The provision allowed 10% of income to be deducted, subject to a cap of $3,000. This deduction was an imperfect device that partly alleviated the problem of the marriage penalty and, for individuals below the cap, reduced the marginal tax rate on the secondary worker. It was repealed in 1986, when the flatter rate structure caused the marriage penalty to be less severe. The marriage penalty was increased for very high-income individuals in 1993 with the addition of higher tax rates. These changes affected, however, only a very small fraction of the population.

The degree of progression in the rate structure interacts to affect the tax burden that applies to taxpayers in different circumstances. The rate structure has varied significantly over time, but a major revision in the 1986 act reduced the brackets to two (15 and 28%) as well as lowering the top bracket. Certain benefits were phased out. In 1990, the "bubble" due to these phaseouts was eliminated in exchange for adding a new tax rate of 31%.[9] (Capital gains were held to a 28% rate). However, personal exemptions were still phased out. Itemized deductions were also phased out, on a temporary basis, reduced by 3% of adjusted gross income (AGI) above a limit. Because itemized deductions tend to rise with income faster than the reductions due to the phaseout, this phaseout is the equivalent of increasing taxable income by 3%, and an additional percentage point or so in tax. (Each dollar of adjusted gross income taxed leads to a reduction in deductions of $0.03, and if the marginal tax rate is around a third, then the additional tax per dollar of income is around $0.01). In 1993, two marginal tax rates were added at the upper income levels, 36% and 39.6%; this legislation made the itemized deduction and personal exemption phaseouts permanent.

The 2001 tax cut, in addition to lowering the top tax rates and introducing a new 10% rate, eliminated the marriage penalty for most taxpayers by increasing the standard deduction, new 10% rate bracket, and the 15% rate bracket to make these values twice as large as for singles, returning to the pre-1969 treatment for most taxpayers. That tax cut also prospectively eliminated the personal exemption phaseout (to begin in 2006 and be complete in 2010) and the itemized deduction phaseout (in 2010).

Earned Income Tax Credit

The earned income tax credit (EIC) is a refundable credit (or negative tax) that provides a wage subsidy for low-income working individuals. The credit is a percentage of earned income, which reaches a maximum fixed amount and then is eventually phased out. The credit rates are currently 7.65% for families without children, 34% for families with one child, and 40% for families with two children. The phase-out levels are higher for families with children than for those without children. In 2005, the credit reached its maximum value of $399 for families with no children at an income of $5,220; the credit is phased out at incomes between $6,530 and $11,750 for singles and between $8,530 and $13,750 for joint returns. For families with one child, the maximum credit of $2,662 is reached at $7,830; the credit is phased out between $14,370 and $31,030 for single heads and between $16,370 and $33,030 for married couples. For families with two or more children, the maximum credit of $4,400 is reached at $11,000 and is phased out between $14,370 and $35,363 for single heads and between $16,3790 and $37,263 for married couples. These values are indexed for inflation.[10]

Unlike some other provisions, there is no differentiation by family type; rather, the differences depend on the presence of one, two or no children. The EIC plays a role in creating a marriage penalty for lower-income families. If individuals with low earnings marry, the couple's higher combined income may phase out more of the earned income tax credit. At the same time, marriage can reduce taxes if a single individual marries someone with children but with little or no income, because he or she becomes eligible for the larger credit for families with children.

The EIC was first enacted in 1975. This provision provided a refundable tax credit for 10% of earned income, phased out at a rate of 10% of income over $4,000. Because the credit was refundable, individuals who paid no income tax were nevertheless eligible for a benefit. There were a variety of rationales for the EIC: to provide a work incentive, to offset the social security tax burden, and to provide relief for recent price increases in food and fuel. The credit was, however, only allowed to individuals who maintained a household for dependent children; thus, like the major welfare program of the time, AFDC (Aid to Families with Dependent Children), the EIC as originally enacted was not extended to singles and childless couples.

The EIC has been revised in various ways, and in 1990 was differentiated with respect to number of children. In 1993, the credits were increased substantially and a small credit was added for families without children.

The 2001 tax cut expanded the phase-out range for married couples which slightly reduced the marriage penalty in the EIC.

Child or Dependent Care Credit

Another provision allows for credits for paid child care expenses for children under 13 and disabled dependents. A deduction for these costs was first allowed in 1954 and converted to a credit in 1976. The credit is 30% of eligible expenses but is phased down to 20% as income rises from $15,000 to $43,000. Eligible expenses are limited to $3,000 for one child, and $6,000 for two or more children. The credit is available only to single parents or married couples where both parents work and is limited to the smaller earned income. It is not indexed.

Alternative Minimum Tax

The alternative minimum tax (AMT) calculates a tax on a broader income base with a large flat exemption (in 2005, $58,000 for married couples and $40,250 for singles) and at rates of 26% and 28%. If this tax is higher than the regular tax, the difference in tax is added to the taxpayer's liability.

Currently, the AMT does not affect very many taxpayers, but its effects will grow over time unless legislative changes are made, including an increase in the exemption and indexing of the exemptions. Thus far, temporary revisions to limit the scope of the AMT have been enacted, the most recent in December 2010 (P.L. 111-312).

The AMT originated in 1969 as an add-on tax on tax preferences and the most important preference was capital gains. At that time, there was an exclusion for a share of capital gains and the excluded share was taxed under the add-on tax. The add-on tax was eventually paired with and then displaced by the AMT. In 1986 the capital gains preference was ended and the number of individuals affected by the tax, already small, fell further. Over time, however, the coverage of the AMT began to grow as rates increased and because the exemption was not indexed, while exemptions in the regular tax were. The potential coverage was also increased with the 2001 tax cut which cut regular rates but not AMT rates. The focus of preferences has also changed. The preference for capital gains enacted in 1997 and extended in 2003, and for dividends enacted in 2003 was not included in the AMT.

Increasingly the major preference items are personal exemptions and certain itemized deductions. (The child credit was allowed against the AMT after it became clear that failure to do so would push many families onto the tax.) In the middle-income classes, large families will increasingly be affected by the AMT, absent change.[11]

Other Provisions

In addition to these basic provisions—rate structures, personal exemptions, standard allowances, and credits—several other provisions related to family structure are summarized here. First, there are specific provisions that relate to family structure or characteristics. There are additional standard deductions for elderly and blind taxpayers (provisions that give little benefit to high income individuals who tend to itemize deductions). In addition, there is a 15% tax credit for the elderly and disabled that is phased out; because the base for the credit is offset by social security, it tends to benefit elderly and disabled individuals who do not receive social security. Another explicit family tax provision, originally adopted in 1986, is the "kiddie tax," which taxes unearned income of children under the age of 14 at the parents' tax rate; this provision expanded to apply to those under the age of 18 in 2006 and under the age of 19 in 2008.

A taxpayer might add a variety of exclusions (some Social Security benefits, welfare payments, in-kind benefits, employer-provided child care) and deductions or credits (medical expenses, educational expenses), which benefit families of certain income levels and characteristics. Moreover, because the tax law does not apply to certain imputed income, families who prefer owner-occupied homes or in-home provision of goods and services, or the consumption of leisure over other goods, have greater tax benefits. These benefits are, in some cases, associated with family characteristics. For example, families with higher incomes and at certain ages are more likely to live in owner-occupied homes. One-earner married couples benefit from the services provided in the home by the non-working spouse, which are not subject to tax.[12]

Finally, the payroll tax can alter the relative net tax burden between different types of families with consequences that could matter for concerns of equity and efficiency (such as work choice). The Social Security system may confer a marriage bonus, that can increase the implicit tax on work effort for second earners. Spouses receive a benefit, without necessarily paying any payroll taxes of their own; a second-earner spouse pays additional social security taxes but his or her benefit is only the net of a benefit based on the individual earnings record and the benefit for spouses—and this amount may not be positive. That is, the spouse's benefit based on the partner's earning record may be better than the benefit a spouse receives on his or her own earnings record, and there is, therefore, no return to payroll taxes paid. Thus, the net tax on a second-earner spouse is effectively larger than it would be in the absence of a benefit for spouses, because little or no additional benefits occur as a result of those payments. There are also implicit taxes that affect behavior in the transfer system, where increases in income through work or marriage may cause a reduction in benefits, thereby discouraging these behaviors.

EQUITY AND DISTRIBUTIONAL ISSUES

Tax proposals can be evaluated on many grounds, but one issue is that of fairness. This issue of fairness can involve two elements: vertical equity, or the equity of changes in tax burdens as income rises for an otherwise identical family; and horizontal equity, or how taxes should be fairly differentiated between families of different sizes and structures. This analysis focuses primarily on the issue of horizontal equity, because this is an issue that can be addressed in a more analytical framework. First, however, the issue of vertical equity is briefly discussed.

Vertical Equity

The individual income tax is progressive in rate structure and in actual outcomes: higher-income taxpayers pay larger shares of their income than do lower-income taxpayers, and at the lowest income levels taxpayers received overall subsidies through the EIC. Because the desired degree of redistribution cannot be easily established, issues of vertical equity involve value judgments to a considerable degree.[13] By and large, the overall distribution of the tax system has not changed a great deal in the past 23 years; all tax rates have fallen and the largest reduction is for the very highest 1% of taxpayers, followed by the middle quintile. At the lower end, the earned income tax credits have more than offset growth in payroll taxes.[14]

How different tax revisions affect the progressivity of the income tax depends on several factors.

First, a significant fraction of taxpayers do not have income tax liability. Positive income taxes do not apply in most cases until individuals are above the poverty line. In the Tax Reform Act of 1986, the combination of standard deductions and personal exemptions were set to roughly approximate the poverty line—the income levels above which families of different sizes are not considered poor. The allowances for single individuals are below the poverty line and cause some poor single individuals to be taxed. The addition of the child credit means that taxpayers with qualifying children well above the poverty line would not be subject to tax. These taxpayers would not be affected by a tax cut.

An exception is when tax cuts are refundable. An expansion of the EIC, which is a refundable credit (or negative tax), would affect low-income individuals. The child credit is also refundable in some circumstances.

Certain types of revisions tend to benefit higher-income individuals, whereas others tend to provide little benefit to that group. For example, although lowering the top rates clearly benefitted higher-income individuals in 2001, it is also clear that widening the 15% rate bracket for joint returns also benefitted higher-income individuals. In 2000, prior to the tax cut, according to the Internal Revenue Service's statistical data, of 129 million returns, approximately 69 million returns paid tax at the 15% rate and another 25 million had no tax liability. Thus, the widening of the 15% bracket, which helped only those paying tax above that rate, benefitted approximately the top 25% of taxpayers. Higher-income individuals are also more likely to itemize deductions, and changes that increase the standard deduction will tend to focus more benefits to moderate-income taxpayers than high-income taxpayers. Similarly, expansions of benefits that are phased out, such as the child credits, would not benefit high-income individuals. The 10% bracket also favored lower-income families.

Horizontal Equity

Horizontal equity has to do with equal treatment of equals and is an important focus of this analysis. For the income tax, this standard might mean that families of the same size with the same income should pay the same tax. But, it could also be taken to mean that two individuals with the same income should pay the same tax. In a progressive tax system, these two standards can be incompatible, and, indeed this incompatibility causes marriage penalties and bonuses in a system where the family is the tax unit. Thus, the basic challenge of assessing standards of horizontal equity is to determine how to treat different taxpayers equitably. First, the economic principles that could be used in that assessment are reviewed. Second, considered in further detail is the ability-to-pay concept, which seems most consistent with the equal-sacrifice principles of horizontal equity.

As the recent history of the tax law suggests and the following discussion reveals, tax policy has not generally been guided by a consistent theory of fairness or equity across different types of families. Indeed, it is clear that many of the structural changes in the treatment of the family were haphazard. Income splitting, perhaps one of the most important aspects of family tax differentials, was adopted in reaction to a legal situation. Other changes were contemporary reactions to a set of complaints or concerns about behavioral response (such as the singles rate schedule or attempts to fix the marriage penalty).

Theories of Equitable Taxation

For taxation purposes, there are two fundamental attributes of families: the type of head (a married couple or a single individual) and the size. Families can be composed of single persons, single parents with children, childless couples, and married couples with children. And, in turn, there are two important features of the tax system that relate to these differences. First, should the unit of taxation be the individual, or the family? The U.S. tax system imposes taxes on families and differentiates in its rate structure between singles, head of households (single parents with children), and married couples. However, an alternative would be to apply a single rate schedule to each individual on his or her own earnings. Although some preference for this view of individual taxation may have to do with philosophical matters, one argument for treating the individual rather than the family as a taxpaying unit has to do with marriage neutrality and efficiency, discussed subsequently. That is, if individuals could be taxed solely on their own earnings, there would be no tax consequences of being married, and the married state would not affect incentives to work via tax differentials.

The second issue is how one should adjust for family size, or, in the case of individual taxation, for the number of dependents. Despite the thrust of recent legislation that added substantial tax credits for children, some of the debate over differentiating by taxpayer characteristics has been over whether personal exemptions for dependents should be allowed at all. Under some theories of how the family should be taxed, no differentiation should be allowed for dependents; indeed, arguments are made that individuals should be taxed on their income without regard to their family arrangements. For that matter, individual taxation does not preclude allowances for number of dependents; rather, its focus is on treating working adults, even though married, as separate entities.[15] (In practice, such a tax system must always deal with the possibility of income splitting of capital income by transfers of assets within the family, as well as the allocation of deductions.)

Clearly, the family involves a social and economic unit that differs from unrelated groupings. Although taxation of the family has received limited attention in the economics literature, various principles have been advanced about how to treat family characteristics. Three such approaches are outlined here: treating living arrangements and children as personal choices that should not be addressed by the tax law, equating post-tax standards of living for families with the same pretax standard of living, and family assistance.

This analysis does not consider another alternative principle of taxation, the benefit principle, which would set taxes to reflect the amount of government services received. It could be argued that large families, particularly families with children, are greater beneficiaries of public spending, such as education. Although some taxes are explicitly formulated as benefit taxes (e.g., the gasoline tax that is used to build roads), the individual income tax has generally been based on other principles, such as the ones described here.

Family Arrangements as Personal Choices

People are relatively free to choose whether to marry and have children, and an argument can be made that such choices should not lead to tax relief. From this perspective, if they choose to have children, they are not worse off, because the enjoyment they receive from their children outweighs any cost. Thus, one could think of children as part of the consumption of the parents.[16] At a minimum, this approach suggests that no allowance be made for the additional cost of supporting children, treating the choice to have children as a consumption item, no different from the decision to consume food or clothing. Similarly, the choice of a spouse could be seen as a consumption or investment choice, which should not alter the tax paid by the individual or the combined tax of the two spouses. In this case, the individual should be the tax unit.

Although the argument that children constitute consumption to their parents may be a defensible one, using this view as a guide to making tax policy is problematic. Even if the adults have made a choice, a troublesome aspect of this treatment of children as consumption is that it considers only the well-being of the parent or parents. Parents' tastes for children aside, the material level of consumption for children as well as for adults is affected by the number of others in the family.

Some theories have suggested that children could be seen as an investment, perhaps for support in old age. There is some justification for this theory of parental motivation, although it must surely be less than universal because many parents leave bequests to their children, rather than being supported by them in old age. If investment were the objective of having children, then there would be some justification for tax relief, because the cost of such an investment should, in theory, be recovered; at the same time, returns (such as help in old age) should be taxed to the parents. Our tax system is not designed along these lines, and, in any case, the children-as-investment theory also suffers from a lack of focus on the well-being of the children.

Ability to Pay Approaches

Another approach is simply that of ability to pay, which is the cornerstone of progressive taxation. Applying this ability-to-pay standard of taxation is straightforward in theory if one begins with the proposition that families with equal standards of living before tax should have equal standards of living after tax. If all family members were more or less identical in their needs and if all goods consumed were purely private in nature, this standard would suggest full income splitting of total family income among all members of the family. Merely, all family income could be divided evenly and then subject each share to an identical rate structure. In a progressive tax system, larger families would pay smaller taxes than smaller families with the same total income.

One difficulty with this straightforward prescription is the existence of "club" goods within the family. Some goods are more or less purely private goods, such as food. If one person consumes food, it is not available to anyone else. Other goods have elements of a club nature (one person can consume the good without interfering with another's consumption). Such club goods include housing and some furnishings, reading materials, and the family car. None of these goods are pure shared goods because individual preferences may not be identical and congestion may occur, but they do provide scale advantages in consumption within a family. These scale advantages in family consumption are recognized in construction of the poverty line, which varies with family size, yet does not increase in full proportion to it.

Another problem is that adults and children may differ in the amount of private goods they need or desire.

If how to scale ability to pay by family size and characteristics were known, design of the income tax would be theoretically straightforward. The method would be as follows. Choose a representative family (e.g., a family of two). Devise the tax rate schedule to achieve the desired degree of progression, setting the exempt level at the poverty level or whatever other level is desired. The solution to horizontal equity is then, simply, an averaging approach. For example, consider a larger family that needs 50% more income than the basic reference family. This means that a larger family that has $75,000 of income should have the same average tax rate as a smaller (reference) family with $50,000 of income. Simply apply the basic tax rate schedule to two thirds of the larger family's income and multiply the resulting tax liability by 1.5. This approach will produce the same effective tax rate for the larger family as for the reference family. (The larger family, which has more income, will still pay more taxes, but the fraction paid will be the same as the smaller family.) The two families will have the same (although smaller) standard of living after tax just as they had the same standard of living before tax.

When exempt levels of tax are set roughly at the poverty rate, as was the intent of the 1986 Tax Reform Act, families whose income falls within the first rate bracket (the 15% tax bracket at that point) tend to have equal effective tax rates, if the relative poverty measures across families are correct (ignoring the earned income tax credit). These effects will not hold, however, when higher-income families are considered or when other provisions, such as the child credit and the earned income credit, are considered, or with a new small bracket such as the 10% bracket introduced in 2001. Moreover, families with one earner are better off than families with two earners at the same income because of the expenses of working, including child care, and the benefits of home production of the non-working spouse. Thus, credits for child care expenses or allowances for working spouses can move the system towards more equitable treatment, at least vis-a-vis one-earner couples.

Targeted Family Assistance

At the opposite end of the spectrum is the notion of targeted family assistance, especially for lower-income families, and often targeted towards children. To accomplish this targeting, allowances for family size differentials (e.g., personal allowances) are often made refundable, they take the form of a credit rather than an exemption, and benefits are often phased out as incomes rise. Several of these features, including the EIC and the child credit, have made their way into current law.

This view of family allowances differs from the philosophy that personal exemptions, along with other exclusions, should be used to exempt a minimum subsistence amount from the income base, the philosophy underlying the 1986 revisions, and one which is more in line with the ability to pay standard. Similarly, a benefit for child care would be more appropriately made through a deduction, if child care was viewed as one of the costs of working under an ability-to-pay approach.

Proposals that are driven by this philosophy are often simultaneously addressing differentiation across family types and a vertical distribution objective. This objective is not necessarily inconsistent with the ability-to-pay objective addressed previously, even though it often appears to be because of the mechanisms chosen, such as credits that are phased out. For a given family size, any degree of vertical equity can be obtained through either exemptions or credits or by arranging the tax rate schedule appropriately. But, the differentiation across families at the same income level (or ability-to-pay) can be achieved only by selecting the sizes of personal exemptions for different family members. An ability-to-pay approach would include differentiation of families of different sizes at either high or low income levels. When a vanishing exemption or credit is chosen in the interest of vertical equity, the actual result is to allow no differentiation for family size at higher-income levels.[17]

Finally, it is important to recognize that the income tax system exists side by side with a welfare system and many conclude that targeted family assistance might better be addressed through the welfare system.

APPLYING THE ABILITY-TO-PAY HORIZONTAL EQUITY STANDARD TO CURRENT LAW

The ability-to-pay approach seems the most consistent and, to many, appealing of the three approaches to dealing with tax differentiation based on family size. This method considers the welfare of all in society rather than focusing exclusively on adults or children. One study used this approach to estimate effective tax rates in 2005, and how various provisions of the tax law affected these rates, using an equivalency scale similar to the variations in poverty lines across family types.[18] Because the tax system has been indexed, the findings of this study remain applicable although income levels refer to 2005 values (excluding temporary provisions but including the alternative minimum income tax patch).

The remainder of this section reports the results of that study. In defining families that have the same ability to pay, an adjustment based on a research study similar to that adjusting for official poverty levels for different family sizes was used, which has a smaller adjustment for children than for adults. Under this standard, a single person requires about 62% of the income of a married couple; a couple with four kids requires about three times the income. Thus, for a married couple with no children with $20,000 of income, an equivalent single person would need slightly over $12,000 and a married couple with four children would need $60,000.

Table 1 reports the 2005 effective tax rates for low- and middle-income taxpayers at different levels of income, for family sizes of up to seven individuals, and for the three basic types of returns—single, joint, and head of household, without considering the child credit. *Table 2* reports the tax rates for higher-income families. The column heading indicates the income level for married couples. Families in each column have the same estimated ability to pay, so that larger families have more income and singles and a head of household with one child have less. The rates across families should be compared by looking down the columns. For example, in *Table 1*, a married couple with $25,000 in income pays 3.4% of income in taxes, but a married couple with one child with the same ability to pay receives a subsidy of 0.7%, whereas a single with an equivalent before tax standard of living pays 4.7%.

These numbers assume that dependents are children eligible for the child credit and that the families are eligible for the earned income tax credit (a provision not allowed for those over the age of 65 or for those without children under the age of 25). These are illustrative calculations that do not account for any other tax preferences and are designed to show how the basic structural, family-related features of the tax law affect burdens. Tax rates for returns paying the AMT are bolded.

These tables suggest that the pattern of tax burden by family size varies across the income scale, as it reflects the complications of the earned income tax credit, the child credit, and graduated rates, including phase-out effects. Moreover, the variation across families that have the same ability to pay is substantial. At low incomes, families with children, whether headed by a married couple or a single parent, are favored because of the earned income tax credit. The largest negative tax rates tend to accrue to returns with two children, because the largest EICs are available for these returns.

As incomes rise, families with children are still favored, but it is the largest families that have the largest subsidies or the smallest tax rates, because of the combination of the personal exemptions and the child credit lower taxes so much for these families.

Table 1. Average Effective Income Tax Rates by Type of Return, Family Size, and Income: Lower and Middle Incomes (2005 tax law and income levels)

Type-Size	Income Level for Married Couple			
	$10,000	$15,000	$25,000	$50,000
Single - 1	-6.5%	-1.0%	4.7%	9.0%
Joint - 2	-2.9	0.0	3.4	8.3
Joint - 3	-23.2	-17.9	-0.7	6.6
Joint - 4	-34.0	-22.4	-2.4	5.3
Joint - 5	-31.4	-18.9	-3.5	4.3
Joint - 6	-27.5	-16.3	-4.8	3.5
Joint - 7	-24.5	-14.3	-6.2	3.0
H/H - 2	-29.8	-22.6	-6.8	6.4
H/H - 3	-39.2	-27.6	-7.9	4.7
H/H - 4	-35.2	-22..7	-5.2	3.7
H/H - 5	-30.8	-18.5	-6.0	4.9
H/H - 6	-26.7	-15.8	-7.4	6.3
H/H - 7	-23.5	-13.7	-8.6	7.4

Source: Gravelle and Gravelle.

Note: The dollar amounts refer to the income for a married couple with no children; larger families in each column would have more income and singles and heads of household with 2 family members (one child) would have less income.

Eventually, large families began to be penalized because the value of the child credit and personal exemptions relative to income declines and larger families that require more income are pushed up through the rate brackets. That effect is increased because more families with children are subjected to the AMT. At higher-income levels, credits and exemptions begin to be phased out. As incomes reach very high levels, however, the rates converge as the tax becomes large a flat tax. (Note that itemized deductions assumed to be a constant fraction of income, and so is a proportional exclusion).

Overall, these calculations suggest (1) that singles are taxed more heavily than childless couples in the middle-income ranges but less heavily at very high and very low income levels; (2) when the child credit and EIC are available, families with children tend to be favored over families without children at low and moderate income levels; (3) the number of children in a family sometimes causes more beneficial treatment and sometimes less depending on how the EIC and child credit are being phased out; and (4) the graduated rate structure causes large families at higher-income levels to be taxed significantly more, an effect exacerbated by the AMT.

Table 2. Average Effective Income Tax Rates by Type of Return, Family Size, and Income: Higher Incomes (2005 tax law and income levels)

Type-Size		Income Level for a Married Couple of Two		
	$75,000	$100,000	$250,000	$500,000
Single - 1	10.5%	12.8%	17.8%	24.2%
Joint - 2	9.5	11.2	19.4	24.8
Joint - 3	8.6	11.9	21.8	24.9
Joint - 4	8.6	12.5	23.4	25.0
Joint - 5	9.0	14.0	24.4	25.1
Joint - 6	10.3	15.5	24.7	25.4
Joint - 7	11.4	16.7	24.8	25.6
H/H - 2	8.9	12.4	21.3	24.6
H/H - 3	9.7	13.6	23.6	24.9
H/H - 4	11.2	15.7	24.3	25.0
H/H - 5	12.6	17.6	24.5	25.3
H/H - 6	13.8	18.9	24.6	25.6
H/H - 7	15.1	19.9	24.7	25.9

Source: Gravelle and Gravelle.

Note: The dollar amounts refer to the income for a married couple with no children; larger families in each column would have more income and singles and heads of household with 2 family members (one child) would have less income.

These results can be characterized as resulting from the fundamental structural flaws of phase-out provisions and rate brackets. Phase-out points and rate brackets should be based on family size if the ability to pay criterion is being used to determine the tax structure. The flat amount of the child credit and personal exemption also causes them to have little effect on relative tax liabilities at high income levels; phasing them out increases the over-taxation of large families relative to small ones at higher-income levels.

At low-income levels, however, the family comparisons are affected by the earned income tax credit, and differences in tax burdens by family size can be striking. If there were no earned income tax credit, effective tax rates would be relatively uniform at the lower-income levels, at zero or a small positive percentage amount. The EIC introduces disparities. First, the EIC rate is much lower for single taxpayers or two-member joint returns where there are no qualifying children than it is for families with children. Second, if one accepts the ability-to-pay standard, the EIC has an inappropriate adjustment for family size. There is no reason to vary the rate of the EIC by family size; but the base (or maximum creditable wage) and the phase-out levels should be varied according to the ability-to-pay standard. That is, both dollar amounts—the amount on which the EIC applies and the income at which the phaseout begins—should be tied to family size according to the ability-to-pay standard, whereas the EIC rate should be the same for all families.

To make the EIC neutral across families, using the ability-to-pay standard, would require, in addition to allowing it at a common rate for all families, changing the base levels and the phaseout levels for family size. Changing the rate, as was done in 1990 and retained when the EIC was expanded in 1993, does not accomplish equal treatment across families of different sizes, providing too much adjustment for some families and not enough for others.

The analysis also considered the effects of other aspects of the tax system. One is the availability of the child care credit. The analysis in that paper indicated that including the child credit (at the maximum) does not have very important effects. The dependent care credit is not effectively available to low-income families who do not have sufficient tax liability to use the credit, and is capped and unimportant in a relative sense for high-income taxpayers. In the middle-income levels, it lowers the tax rate for families with children.

Another issue has to do with the treatment of married couples where only one individual works outside the home. These families are better off because the spouse not employed outside the home can perform services at home that result in cost savings, perform household tasks that increase leisure time for the rest of the family, or enjoy leisure. The value of this time, which is not counted in the measured transactions of the economy, is referred to as "imputed income." This imputed income is not taxed, and it would probably be impractical to tax it. Nevertheless, the tax burden as a percentage of cash plus imputed income is lower for such a family.

Imputed income is not easily valued and this issue is explored in the study by limiting the imputed income to the value of child care using the cap for the expenses eligible for a child care credit and excluding this amount from income. For low-income families, this change actually increased taxes by reducing earned income credits. At moderate and middle incomes, it benefitted married couples with children, who already tend to be favored.

The authors also considered some of the potential changes and whether those changes would increase horizontal equity or exacerbate it. In the interest of increased horizontal equity, the analysis would support an increase in the earned income credit for those without children; a reduction (or containment) of the AMT, which will grow in importance absent change; and an elimination of phaseouts for child credits, personal exemptions, and itemized deductions. (2001 tax law changes proposed to eliminate the phaseout of the latter two beginning in 2007.) Making the child credit fully refundable would increase disparities in tax rates at the lower-income levels.

These calculations should be considered with caution, as they depend on the precision of the family equivalency scales, which do not take into account the heterogeneity of the cost of rearing children, and are aimed at measuring cash needs to attain a given standard of living. Lower-income families with younger children who need child care may find their standard of living in material matters lower than other types of families, because of the higher cost of that care relative to their income. In that case, the lower rates due to child care credits or exclusion of imputed income may be appropriate. At higher-income levels, child care costs are probably much smaller relative to income, even if more is spent on care. The child care credit, however, has little effect on effective tax rates at these income levels.

MARRIAGE PENALTIES AND MARRIAGE BONUSES

Concerns about the marriage penalty reflect a reluctance to penalize marriage in a society that upholds such traditions. As the tax law shifts to reduce the marriage penalty, as it did in 2001, it also expands marriage bonuses. These choices have consequences not only for incentives but for equitable treatment of singles and married couples. As shown above in *Table 1* and *Table 2*, in the middle-income brackets, where the marriage penalty was largely eliminated, singles with the same ability to pay are subject to higher taxes than married couples. Singles benefit at lower-income levels because their lower required incomes do not phase them out of the earned income credit. And at very high incomes married couples may pay a larger share of their income because of marriage penalties that remain in the AMT and the upper brackets of the rate structure.

This section explores the treatment of married couples and singles in an additional dimension by assuming that singles live together and share the same economies of scale that married couples do. These individuals could be room mates, but they could also be partners who differ from married couples only in that they are not legally married.[19] Single individuals who live together in the same fashion as married couples have the same ability to pay with the same income. However, remaining single can alter their tax liability. Remaining single can cause tax liability either to rise or fall, depending on the split of income between the two spouses. If one individual earns most of the income, tax burdens will be higher for two individuals who are not married than for a married couple with the same total income, because the standard deductions are smaller and the rate brackets narrower. If income is evenly split between the two individuals, there can be a benefit from remaining single. Married individuals have to combine their income, and the rate brackets for joint returns at the higher-income brackets, whereas wider than those for single individuals, are not twice as wide. At all levels they are not wider than those for heads of household.

The marriage penalty or bonus might, in the context of the measures of household ability to pay, also be described as a singles bonus or penalty. In any case, in considering both the incentive and equity dimension to this issue, the tax rates of these families should be compared with the tax rates of other households.

Table 3 and *Table 4* show the effective tax rates for married couples and for unmarried couples with the same combined income, both where income is evenly split and where all income is received by one person. In one case there is no child and in the other a single child. These income splits represent the extremes of the marriage penalty and the marriage bonus. The same reference income classes and equivalency scales in *Table 1* and *Table 2* are used.

Note that uneven income splits in the case of a family with a child can yield different results depending on whether the individual with the income can claim the child and therefore receive the benefits of the head of household rate structure, the higher earned income credit, the dependency exemption, and the child credit. If not, that individual files as a single.

The tables indicate that both marriage penalties and bonuses persist. In the case of families without children, however, penalties do not exist in the middle-income ranges, only bonuses. In this case, singles who live together and who have uneven incomes would see their tax rates fall if they got married. Both bonuses and penalties exist at the lower-income levels because of the earned income tax credit. If income is evenly split, the phaseout ranges are not reached as quickly for singles because each of the partners has only half the income. If all of the income is earned by one of the singles in the single partnership, phaseout of the credit still occurs and the individual also has a smaller standard deduction, and thus pays a higher tax. The smaller deductions and narrower rate brackets also cause the higher tax rates through the middle-income brackets. At very high-income levels, marriage penalties can also occur. Some of the penalty is due to not doubling the rate brackets after the 15% bracket, but more of it is due to the marriage penalties in the AMT. If there were no AMT, tax rates for joint returns would be 17.1% and 22.8% for the $250,000 and $500,000 incomes. The regular tax is still responsible for most of the penalty for singles with one partner earning income: the regular rates are 20.9% and 24.1% for the $250,000 and $500,000 incomes.

Table 3. Average Effective Income Tax Rates for Joint Returns and Unmarried Couples, by Size of Income and Degree of Split: Lower and Middle Incomes (2005 Levels of Income)

Type-Size	Income Level for Married Couple			
	$10,000	$15,000	$25,000	$50,000
No Child				
Joint	-2.9	0.0	3.4	8.3
Single 50/50 Split	- 7.7	- 4.3	3.4	6.6
Single 100/0 Split	0.5	4.5	8.3	11.2
One Child				
Joint	-23.2	-17.9	-0.7	6.6
50/50 Split One Single, One Head of Household	-19.9	-15.0	-7.9	6.1
100/0 Split, Single Return	3.5	6.4	9.0	12.8
100/0 Split, Head of Household Return	-23.2	-13.6	3.3	8.0

Source: Congressional Research Service.
Note: Effective tax rate does not always rise across incomes due to rounding.

Matters are more complex for families with one child. At low-income levels, and a 50/50 split, one of the singles files a single return with a very limited negative rate because of the small earned income credit for those without children, while the other claims a child and has a much higher negative tax rate than a married couple because there is no phaseout of benefits. The result is that there is a marriage bonus. This eventually becomes a marriage penalty because of the favorable head of household standard deduction and rate structure. The penalty continues through all the incomes shown, although it eventually becomes very small at the top. A small part of this penalty is due to the AMT at the $250,000 equivalent incomes: the rates without the AMT for a joint return is 19.7% and the rate for the combined singles 16.8%. Eliminating the AMT would, however, widen the discrepancy between the two at the $500,000 equivalent level: without the AMT the rates would be 23.9% for a joint return and 21.6% for the combined singles.

Table 4. Average Effective Income Tax Rates for Joint Returns and Unmarried Couples, by Size of Income and Degree of Split: Higher Incomes (2005 Levels of Income)

Type	Income Level for Married Couple			
	$75,000	$100,000	$250,000	$500,000
No Child				
Joint	9.5 %	11.2 %	19.4 %	24.8 %
Single 50/50 Split	9.5	11.2	16.7	22.4
Single 100/0 Split	14.0	15.5	22.4	24.8
One Child				
Joint	8.6	11.9	21.8	24.9
50/50 Split One Single, One Head of Household	8.5	10.4	17.6	24.2
100/0 Split, Single Return	15.0	16.6	24.2	25.0
100/0 Split, Head of Household Return	12.1	14.6	24.2	25.0

Source: Congressional Research Service.
Note: Effective tax rate does not always rise across incomes due to rounding.

With one of the pair earning all of the income, the results depend on whether the partner with the income can claim the child. If that person cannot, the tax burden is higher throughout the scale (although it reaches roughly the same level at the highest level in part because of the AMT). The discrepancy at the $250,000 level is increased slightly by the AMT (the regular rates are 19.7% for the joint return and 22.1% for the single). If the person with the income can claim the child, joint returns are still favored, but not by nearly as much. Which of these last two assumptions seems more likely depends on the circumstances. When couples divorce, they typically move to different residences and the most usual outcome is that the mother who typically has lower earnings would have the child. According to the Census Bureau, 83% of children who live with one parent live with their mother.[20] In that case, the comparisons in *Table 1* and *Table 2* would be appropriate. If the couple divorce but live together, presumably the higher-income spouse would claim the child. However, if a couple never married and the child is only related to one parent, that person, more likely the mother and more likely to have low income, would claim the child. If such a couple married and had low incomes, they could obtain the earned income credit and a study of low-income families indicates that this latter effect, the bonus, is the most common effect of the EIC.[21]

Which circumstances are more characteristic of the economy? Note first that, although people refer to the marriage penalty for a particular family situation or the aggregate size of the marriage penalty, it is really not possible, in many cases, to determine the size of the penalty or bonus. The effect of assignment of a child is demonstrated in *Table 3* and *Table 4*, but other features matter. Only when a married couple has only earned income, no dependent children, and no itemized deductions or other special characteristics, and only if it is assumed that their behavior would not have been different if their marital status had been different, can one actually measure the size of the marriage penalty or bonus. There is no way to know who would have custody of the children and therefore which of the partners might be eligible for head of household status and for the accompanying personal exemptions and child credits.

There is reason to expect that unmarried individuals are penalized in the aggregate. Prior to the 2001 tax cut, which increased bonuses and reduced penalties, using an allocation that reflects typical behavior of married couples with respect to child custody, the Congressional Budget Office (CBO) estimated that 37% of married couples had penalties ($24 billion), 3% were unaffected, and 60% had bonuses ($73 billion). (Itemized deductions and earned income were assigned in proportion to earnings). The net bonus was $49 billion.[22] However, in most of its analysis, the CBO study relied on a measure of marriage penalties and bonuses that assumed child custody would be based on a tax-minimizing strategy. For example, if parents of two children had similar individual earnings, each would be assumed to have custody of one of the children so that both would be eligible for head-of-household status. Even using that standard, net bonuses occurred: 43% of married couples had penalties amounting to $32 billion, and 52% had bonuses of $43 billion, for a net bonuses of $11 billion. Nevertheless, a significant proportion of married taxpayers—between 37% and 43%—paid marriage penalties.

A study using Treasury data and other assumptions produced different measures of the marriage bonus or penalty.[23] Using an assumption that divorced parents occupied the same residence, and thus only one could qualify for head of household status, the authors found that 48% had a penalty ($28.3 billion) and 41% had a bonus ($26.7 billion), for a net penalty of $1.6 billion. This study also provided several other ways of measuring penalties and bonuses, including estimating $30.2 billion in singles penalties because these individuals could not use joint return rate schedules. Some of the penalty applied to families with children because of the benefits of head of household status. Without head-of-household status, the Treasury found that 46% of couples have bonuses ($36.6 billion), 43% had penalties ($20.8 billion) and the net effect was a bonus of $15.8 billion.

Treasury researchers did a subsequent study using the standard assumption for the effects of the 2001 tax cut and for 2004 income levels.[24] As before, they essentially found a penalty (of $3.7 billion) without the 2001 tax cut, but found a $30 billion bonus with 2004 tax law (which included explicit marriage relief provisions and other provisions such as rate reductions). About 60% of couples have bonuses, and 23% have penalties (while some have no effect). The study also warns that penalties will grow substantially if the AMT continues to grow as projected.

Given the shift away from penalties and towards bonuses in 2001, it seems clear that the current situation is characterized by bonuses rather than penalties. However, if the AMT is allowed to grow and begins to cover many taxpayers, more significant penalties will return.

An alternative measurement is the bonuses and penalties of single individuals who are cohabitating, a much smaller group of people. In 2005, according to the Census Bureau, there were 58 million married households, but only 5 million unmarried couple households (with partners of the opposite sex).[25] (There were 77 million households altogether.) Thus, assuming that these households were similar to married households, the "single penalties and bonuses" measured by looking at unmarried cohabitating households would be about 9% of the size of "marriage bonuses and penalties" measured by looking at married households.

A study has been made of penalties and bonuses for existing co-habiting couples with children, which assign the children to the biological parent, or, if both partners are biological parents to the higher earner.[26] This study found that under 2003 law, 42% of these couples would experience a bonus averaging $1,893 whereas 50.7% would experience a penalty of $1,497. Under 2003 law, 48.5% receive an average bonus of $2,236 and 44.1% receive a penalty of $1,513. Bonuses are actually more prevalent in low-income households because marriage often increases the earned income credit.

In general, therefore, the rules tend to indicate that singles who are living together are, on average, being penalized relative to married couples, but this pattern does not hold for all circumstances.

The marriage penalty cannot be easily addressed because the tax rules cannot simultaneously achieve three apparently desired income tax objectives: a progressive tax, a marriage neutral tax, and equal treatment of couples with the same total incomes, but with different income shares. Moreover, even if horizontal equity were chosen, the achievement of that system would require information on living arrangements of unmarried individuals that is not available to the tax authorities. The current system, however, appears to lean toward benefitting marriage, as long as the AMT is contained.

CONCLUSION

The analysis of equity across families suggests that, based on an ability to pay standard, families with children are paying lower rates of tax (or receiving larger negative tax rates) than single individuals and married couples at lower and middle incomes, while families with children are being taxed more heavily at higher-income levels. At the lowest income levels, the EIC provides the largest tax subsidies to single parents with two children, followed by single parents with three children and married couples with two children. The smallest subsidies go to childless couples, but all families with children have much larger subsidies than either childless couples or single individuals. At middle-income levels, families with many children will have the most favorable treatment because of the effect of the child credit, which has a very large effect relative to tax liability. At higher-income levels, large families are penalized because the adjustments for children such as personal exemptions and child credits are too small or are phased out, while graduated rates cause larger families that need more income to maintain a given living standard to pay higher taxes. Tax rates are more variable at lower-income levels. At all but the lowest and highest income levels, singles pay higher taxes than married couples.

After the 2001 tax cut, the vast majority of taxpayers without children receive a marriage bonus rather than a penalty, with penalties occurring only at the bottom and at the top—the latter due largely to the AMT. The comparison of families with children is less easily defined. Overall, marriage appears to be rewarded, but if the AMT continues to increase its scope (as it will absent legislation) penalties will begin to reach back in the middle-income classes.

H.R. 3970, introduced by Chairman Rangel of the Ways and Means Committee in the 110th Congress, included a number of changes that would have effects on relative tax treatment of family types. It would double the size of the earned income tax credit for single individuals without children, which would narrow the differences between family types at the lower-income levels. It would also increase the refundability of the child credit, benefitting lower-income families with children, although the cost of that change is smaller. It would also slightly increase the standard deduction, with relative increases designed not to increase the marriage penalty, but which would, based on ability to pay, favor married couples. At the higher end of the scale it would restore phaseouts of itemized deductions, which would maintain some unevenness across family types but also would repeal the AMT, which penalizes families with children at higher-income levels.

Temporary provisions considered as part of the American Recovery and Reinvestment Act of 2009 (H.R. 1 and S. 1) provide additional tax reductions especially to lower-income individuals. The increase in the refundability of the child credit, which was extended for two years (through 2012) by P.L. 111-312, increases the favorable treatment of lower-income families with children.

End Notes

[1] See CRS Report RL34249, *The Tax Reduction and Reform Act of 2007: An Overview*, by Jane G. Gravelle, for an overview of the provisions of H.R. 3970.

[2] The ratio of prices in 2005 to those in 1948 using the GDP deflator is 7.03, while personal exemptions have increased from $600 to $3200, a ratio of 5.33.

[3] In general, floors and ceilings for standard deductions for joint returns were halved for married couples filing separate returns.

[4] In 2005, the personal exemption was $3,200 and the standard deduction $10,000, for a total of $22,800. The exempt allowance in 1948 was $2,667 (600 times 4 divided by 0.9). If the 1948 levels had kept pace with the GDP deflator, the total amount would be $20,177.

[5] Kyle Mudry and Michael Parisi, Individual Income Tax Rates and Shares, Internal Revenue Service *Statistics of Income Bulletin*, 2003, posted at http://www.irs.ustreas.gov/ taxstats/ indtaxstats/article/0,,id=129270,00.html#_article.

[6] Details of the tax rates can be found in CRS Report RL30007, *Individual Income Tax Rates: 1989 through 2007*, by Gregg A. Esenwein.

[7] The itemized deduction phase-out range, which is indexed for inflation, begins at $145,950 for 2005; the personal exemption phaseout, which is also indexed, varies by type of return, but

begins at about $145,950 for singles. The top rate of 35% begins at $326,450 of *taxable income*. Child credits begin to phase out at about $75,000 for head of household returns and $110,000 for joint returns.

[8] Internal Revenue Service, *Statistics of Income*, posted at http://www.irs.ustreas.gov/ taxstats/ indtaxstats/article/0,,id=96981,00.html#_grp1.

[9] Although there were two statutory rate brackets after 1986, 15% and 28%, there was also a surcharge that was designed to phase out the benefits of the 15% rate and the personal exemptions for high income taxpayers. This surcharge effectively increased the tax rate by 5 percentage points, to 33%, and created a bubble: rates were 15%, then 28%, then 33%, and then fell back to 28%.

[10] See CRS Report RS21352, *The Earned Income Tax Credit (EITC): Changes for 2009 and 2010*, by Christine Scott.

[11] For a more detailed discussion and history, see CRS Report RL30149, *The Alternative Minimum Tax for Individuals*, by Steven Maguire.

[12] This concept be may unfamiliar, particularly to readers who think of spouses working at home as making a monetary sacrifice, perhaps to stay with their children. While their income is smaller, they save the taxes that would have been paid on outside earnings. However, these spouses do not give up all of their income, since there are cost savings, as in lower child care payments or not having to pay for other services (e.g., dry cleaning, household help). It is this value that provides a benefit to one-earner families and is the imputed income not subject to tax.

[13] Progressivity in the tax system is typically based on an equal sacrifice notion and the notion that a dollar to a poor person is much more valuable than a dollar to the wealthy person. These theories do not easily pin down the desired degree of progressivity, however. For a more extensive discussion of distributional issues and of the distribution of the income tax see CRS Report RL32693, *Distribution of the Tax Burden Across Individuals: An Overview*, by Jane G. Gravelle.

[14] See Congressional Budget Office, *Historical Effective Federal Tax Rates: 1979 to 2003*, December 2005: http://www.cbo.gov/ftpdoc.cfm?index=7000&type=1.

[15] See Harvey E. Brazer, "Income Tax Treatment of the Family," and Alicia Munnell, "The Couple vs. The Individual under the Federal Personal Income Tax," both in *The Economics of Taxation*, ed. Henry J. Aaron and Michael J. Boskin, Washington, DC, Brookings Institution, 1980.

[16] The notion of children as consumption can be traced to Henry Simons, *Personal Income Taxation* (Chicago: University of Chicago Press, 1938).

[17] One argument along these lines is that progressive taxation could be justified by the need to maintain human resources at the bottom of the scale (which justifies some minimum exclusion) and curb the accumulation of power at the top. Since the accumulation of power is undiminished by family size, there should be little differentiation at the top of the scale. See Harold M. Groves, *Federal Tax Treatment of the Family*, Washington, DC, The Brookings Institution, 1963.

[18] Jane Gravelle and Jennifer Gravelle, "Horizontal Equity and Family Tax Treatment: The Orphan Child of Tax Policy," *National Tax Journal*, vol 59, September 2006, pp. 631-649. This study calculated stylized effective tax rates reflecting personal exemptions, itemized or standard deductions, the child credit, and the earned income credit The equivalency formula used was $(A+0.7K)0.7$ based on Constance F. Citro and Robert T. Michael, *Measuring Poverty: A New Approach*, Washington, DC, National Academy Press, 1995. Using this formula, a single person would need 62% of the income of a married couple without

children to achieve the same standard of income. A married couple with one child would need 23% more and a married couple with two children would need 45% more.

[19] For other discussions of this issue, see Daniel Feenberg, "The Tax Treatment of Married Couples and the 1981 Tax Law," In *Taxing the Family*, Ed. Rudolph G. Penner, Washington: American Enterprise Institute for Public Policy Research, 1983; Harvey Rosen, "The Marriage Tax is Down But Not Out," *National Tax Journal*, Vol. 40, December, 1987, pp 567-576; Daniel R. Feenberg and Harvey S. Rosen." Recent Developments in the Marriage Tax." *National Tax Journal*, Vol. 48, March 1995, pp. 91-101. Rosen, Harvey, "Is It Time to Abandon Joint Filing?" *National Tax Journal*, Vol. 30 (December 1977): 423-428. U.S. Congressional Budget Office. *For Better or for Worse: Marriage and the Federal Income Tax*. Washington, DC, June 1997.

[20] U.S. Census Bureau, Table C2: Household Relationships and Living Arrangements of Children Under 18 http://www.census.gov/population/www/socdemo/hh-fam/cps2005.html.

[21] See Stacy Dickert-Conlin and Scott Houser. "Taxes and Transfers: A New Look at the Marriage Penalty." *National Tax Journal* 51, June 1998, pp. 175-217.

[22] These and other numbers discussed in this paragraph are from an update of a study by the U.S. Congressional Budget Office, *For Better or for Worse: Marriage and the Federal Income Tax*. Washington, DC, June 1997. These numbers were updated for 1999 in a memorandum from Bob Williams and David Weiner of CBO dated September 18, 1998.

[23] Nicholas Bull, Janet Holtzblatt, James R. Nunns, and Robert Rebelein. Assessing Marriage Penalties and Bonuses. *Proceedings of the 91st Annual Conference of the National Tax Association*, 1998, pp. 327-340. An updated version of this paper is published as Office of Tax Analysis Paper 82, Defining and Measuring Marriage Penalties and Bonuses, November 1999 http://www.ustreas.gov/ota/ota82_revised.pdf.

[24] Robert Gillette, Janet Holtzblatt, and Emily Y. Yin, "Marriage Penalties and Bonuses: A Longer Term, Proceeding of the National Tax Association," 2004, Washington, DC, National Tax Association, pp. 468-478.

[25] See http://www.census.gov/population/www/socdemo/hh-fam/cps2005.html.

[26] Elaine Maag, "Taxes and Marriage for Cohabiting Parents," *Tax Notes*, May 23, 2005, p. 1031.

In: Federal Taxes and Families ISBN: 978-1-61942-864-5
Editors: T. I. Owens and R. O. Reynolds ©2012 Nova Science Publishers, Inc.

Chapter 2

THE CHILD TAX CREDIT: CURRENT LAW AND LEGISLATIVE HISTORY[*]

Margot L. Crandall-Hollick

SUMMARY

This report provides background information on the child tax credit. Specifically, the report provides an overview of the child tax credit under current law, as well as a legislative history of this tax benefit, which helps explain its purpose and current structure.

When calculating the total amount of federal income taxes owed, eligible taxpayers can reduce their federal income tax liability (the taxes due after the marginal tax rate schedule is applied to their taxable income) by the child tax credit. Currently, eligible families that claim the child tax credit can subtract up to $1,000 per qualifying child from their federal income tax liability. The maximum amount of credit a family can receive is equal to the number of qualifying children in a family times $1,000. If a family's tax liability is less than the value of their child tax credit, they may be eligible for a refundable credit calculated using the earned income formula. Under this formula, a family is eligible for a refund equal to 15% of their earnings in excess of $3,000, up to the maximum amount of the credit. The credit phases out for single parents with income over $75,000 and married couples with income over $110,000.

---

[*] This is an edited, reformatted and augmented version of a Congressional Research Service publication, CRS Report for Congress R41873, from www.crs.gov, Prepared for Members and Committees of Congress ,dated June 17, 2011.

The child tax credit was created in 1997 by the Taxpayer Relief Act of 1997 (P.L. 105-34) to help ease the financial burden that families incur when they have children. Like other tax credits, the child tax credit reduces tax liability on a dollar for dollar basis. Initially the child tax credit was a nonrefundable credit for most families. A nonrefundable tax credit can only reduce a taxpayer's tax liability to zero, while a refundable tax credit can exceed a taxpayer's tax liability, providing a cash payment to low-income taxpayers who owe little or no tax. Since it was first enacted, the child tax credit has undergone significant changes, most notably by the Economic Growth and Tax Relief Reconciliation Act of 2001 (EGTRRA; P.L. 107-16) and the American Recovery and Reinvestment Act of 2009 (ARRA; P.L. 111-5) which increased the availability of the credit to many low-income families by making the credit partially refundable. The changes made by these laws were extended through the end of 2012 by the Tax Relief, Unemployment Insurance Reauthorization, and Job Creation Act of 2010 (P.L. 111-312). At the end of the 112th Congress, the child tax credit will revert to a $500 per child credit that is nonrefundable for most families if no further extensions occur.

INTRODUCTION

The child tax credit was created in 1997 by the Taxpayer Relief Act of 1997 (P.L. 105-34) to help ease the financial burden that families incur when they have children. Like other tax credits, the child tax credit reduces tax liability on a dollar for dollar basis. Initially the child tax credit was a nonrefundable credit for most families. A nonrefundable tax credit can only reduce a taxpayer's tax liability to zero, while a refundable tax credit can exceed a taxpayer's tax liability, providing a cash payment primarily to low-income taxpayers who owe little or no income tax. Over the past 10 years, legislative changes have significantly changed the credit, transforming it from a nonrefundable credit available only to the middle and upper-middle class, to a partially refundable credit that more low-income families are eligible to claim.

At the end of 2012, the child tax credit is scheduled to return to its original form, a nonrefundable credit available to mostly middle- and upper-middle-income families. Congress may allow the current policy structure of the credit to expire, they may extend current policy, or they may modify different parameters of the credit. This report provides an overview of the credit under current law and examines the legislative history of the credit, reviewing how the credit has changed over the past two decades to provide background to any upcoming debate on the future of this tax benefit.

CURRENT LAW

Currently, the child tax credit allows a taxpayer to reduce their federal income tax liability (the taxes owed before tax credits are applied) by up to $1,000 per child. If the value of the credit exceeds the amount of tax a family owes, the family may be eligible to receive a full or partial refund of the difference. The total amount of their refund is calculated as 15% (the refundability rate) of earnings that exceed $3,000 (the refundability threshold), up to the maximum amount of the credit ($1,000 per child). The credit phases out for higher-income taxpayers. The child tax credit can currently offset a taxpayer's Alternative Minimum Tax (AMT). Key parameters of the child tax credit are scheduled to expire at the end of 2012. Currently, the maximum credit per child, refundability threshold, and phase-out thresholds are not indexed for inflation. *Table 1* provides an overview of key provisions of the child tax credit under current law for tax years 2011, 2012, and beyond.

Table 1. Overview of Key Aspects of the Child Tax Credit under Current Law

Parameter	2011 and 2012	Post 2012
Maximum credit per child	$1,000	$500
Refundability Threshold	$3,000	nonrefundable for most families*
Refundability Rate	15%	nonrefundable for most families*
Phase-out Threshold	$55,000 married separate return $75,000 head of household $110,000 married joint return	same
Phase-out Rate	5%	same
Offset AMT tax liability	YES	NO

Source: Internal Revenue Code, 26 U.S.C. § 24.
Notes: *After 2012, only families with three or more qualifying children will be eligible to claim a refundable credit using the alternative formula. See "Alternative Refundability Formula for Larger Families."

Detailed Overview of Current Credit

For tax years[1] 2011 and 2012, eligible families can claim a child tax credit and reduce their federal income tax liability by up to $1,000 per qualifying child.[2] The maximum amount of credit a family can receive is equal to the number of qualifying children in a family times $1,000. For example, a family with two qualifying children may be eligible for a $2,000 credit. If the value of the family's credit is greater than its actual tax liability, the family may be eligible to receive the difference as a refund. For example, if a family with two eligible children has an income tax liability of $1,000, (which is less than the $2,000 value of their child credit), the family may be able to receive up to $1,000 as a refund, depending on its earnings.

The Earned Income Formula

(two-parent, three-child family with earnings of $20,000)

Earned Income Formula

(earnings - refundability threshold) x (refundability rate)
($20,000 - $3,000) x 15%= $2,550

The total amount of the child tax credit calculated under the earned income formula cannot exceed the maximum allowable credit, which equals $1,000 credit per child multiplied by the number of qualifying children (in this case $3,000).

The refundable portion of the credit, sometimes referred to as the "additional child tax credit" or ACTC, is equal to 15% of the family's earnings in excess of $3,000, up to the maximum credit amount. This formula for calculating the refundable portion of the credit is sometimes referred to as the earned income formula. The earned income formula is scheduled to expire at the end of 2012, limiting the refundability of the credit. The child tax credit is often referred to as a "partially refundable" credit (in contrast to a fully refundable credit like the Earned Income Tax Credit (EITC)). A tax credit is partially refundable if, in cases where the credit is larger than the taxpayer's tax liability, the Internal Revenue Service (IRS) only refunds part of the difference. Families with three or more children are eligible to use another formula to calculate refundability, the alternative formula, which will be discussed further in the next section.

The child tax credit phases out for higher-income families. The $1,000-per-child value of the credit falls by a certain amount as a family's income rises. Specifically, for every $1,000 of modified adjusted gross income (AGI)[3] above a threshold amount, the credit falls by $50. The thresholds depend on a taxpayer's filing status, and are $75,000 for single parents filing as heads of household, $110,000 for married taxpayers filing joint returns, and $55,000 for married taxpayers filing separate returns. The actual income level at which the credit is entirely phased out depends on the number of qualifying children. Generally, it takes $20,000 of modified AGI above the phase-out threshold to completely phase out $1,000 of credit. For example, the credit will completely phase out for a married couple with two children if their modified AGI exceeds $150,000. Currently, the maximum credit amount, the earnings refundability threshold, and the phase-out thresholds are not indexed for inflation. The child tax credit can offset a taxpayer's alternative minimum tax (AMT)[4] through the end of 2012.

Alternative Refundability Formula for Larger Families

Families with three or more children may choose to calculate the refundable portion of the child tax credit using an alternative formula. If the amount calculated under the alternative formula is larger than the refundable credit calculated under the earned income formula, the larger credit can be claimed. The alternative formula is calculated as the excess of a taxpayer's payroll taxes[5] (including one-half of any self-employment taxes) over their earned income tax credit (EITC), not to exceed the maximum credit amount. However, lower-income taxpayers, those in 2011 with earnings below $32,275 or $36,000[6] depending on filing status, will pay less in payroll taxes than they will receive in the EITC.[7] In other words, in 2011 a married couple with three or more children would need to have earnings between $36,000-$43,998[8] to be eligible for a refundable credit under this formula. Since the earned income formula for refundability is scheduled to expire at the end of 2012, the alternative refundability formula will be the only refundability formula available, and it will be limited to families with three or more children.

The Alternative Refundability Formula
(two parent, three child family with earnings of $20,000)
Alternative Formula
(7.65% x earnings) - (EITC) (7.65% x $20,000) - $5,112*
In this example, the taxpayer pays less in payroll taxes, $1,530, than they receive in the EITC, $5,112, and thus does not receive a refundable credit under this formula. In 2011 and 2012, they would use the earned income formula to claim $2,550.

Earned Income vs. Alternative Refundability Formula		
(two parent, three child family with earnings of $20,000)		
	2011 and 2012	Post 2012
Earned Income Formula	$2,550	$0
Alternative Refundability	$0	$0

Definition of a Qualifying Child

In order to claim the child tax credit, a taxpayer's child must be considered "a qualifying child" and meet several requirements which may differ from eligibility requirements for other child-related tax benefits:[9]

- The child must be under 17 years of age during the entire year for which the taxpayer claims the credit (for example, if the child was 16.5 years on December 31, 2010, the taxpayer could claim the credit on their 2010 federal income tax return).
- The child must be claimed as a dependent on the taxpayer's return.
- The child must be the taxpayer's son, daughter, grandson, granddaughter, stepson, stepdaughter, niece, nephew, or an eligible foster child of the taxpayer.
- The child must live with the taxpayer for at least half the year for which the taxpayer wishes to claim the credit.

- The child cannot provide more than half of their own support during the tax year.
- The child must be a U.S. citizen.[10] The statute requires that taxpayers who intend to claim the child tax credit provide a valid Taxpayer Identification Number (TIN) for each qualifying child on their federal income tax return. In most cases, this TIN will be the child's Social Security number.

The age and citizenship requirements for a qualifying child differ from the definition of a qualifying child used for other tax benefits and can cause confusion among taxpayers. For example, a taxpayer's 18-year-old child may meet all the requirements for a qualifying child for the EITC, but will be too old to be eligible for the child tax credit.

LEGISLATIVE HISTORY

The child tax credit was initially structured in the Taxpayer Relief Act of 1997 (P.L. 105-34) as a $500-per-child nonrefundable credit to provide tax relief to middle- and upper-middle-income families. Since 1997, various laws have modified key parameters of the credit, expanding the availability of the benefit to more low-income families while also increasing the value of the tax credit. The first significant change to the child tax credit occurred with the enactment of the Economic Growth and Tax Relief Reconciliation Act of 2001 (EGTRRA; P.L. 107-16). EGTRRA increased the amount of the credit over time to $1,000 per child and made it partially refundable under the earned income formula. For more information on the exact parameter changes see Table 2. Subsequent legislation enacted in 2003 and 2004 accelerated the implementation of the changes made under EGTRRA. In 2008 and 2009, Congress enacted legislation, the Emergency Economic Stabilization Act of 2009 (EESA; P.L. 110-343) and the American Recovery and Reinvestment Act of 2009 (ARRA; P.L. 111-5) which further expanded the availability and amount of the credit to taxpayers whose income was too low to either qualify for the credit or be eligible for the full credit. EESA lowered the refundability threshold to $8,500 in 2008, while ARRA lowered the refundability threshold to $3,000 for 2009 through 2010. The Tax Relief, Unemployment Insurance Reauthorization, and Job Creation Act of 2010 (P.L. 111-312) extended both the EGTRRA provisions of the child tax credit and the expansion of refundability under ARRA for two years through the end of 2012.

Table 2. Changes to the Child Tax Credit Made by Legislation 1997-2010

Parameter	1997	1999	2001	2003	2004	2008	2009	2010
	P.L. 105-34	P.L. 106-170	P.L. 107-16 (EGTRRA)	P.L. 108-27 (JGTRRA)	P.L. 108-311 (WFTRA)	P.L. 110-343 (EESA)	P.L. 111-5 (ARRA)	P.L. 111-312
Maximum Credit per Child	$400 (1998) $500 (after)	*	$600 (2001-04) $700 (2005-08) $800 (2009) $1,000 (2010)	$1,000 (2003-04)	$1,000 (2005-09)	*	*	$1,000 (2011-12)
Inflation adj.	NO	*	*	*	*	*	*	*
Refundable[a]	NO	*	YES (2001-2010)	*	*	*	*	*
Refundability Threshold	na	*	$10,000 (2001-10)	*	*	$8,500 (2008)	$3,000 (2009-10)	$3,000 (2011-12)
Inflation Adj.	na	*	YES (2002-10)	*	*	NO	NO (2009-2010)	NO (2011-12)
Refundability Rate	na	*	10% (2001-04) 15% (2005-10)	*	15% (2004)	*	*	15% (2011-12)
Phase-Out	$55,000 MFS							

	1997	1999	2001	2003	2004	2008	2009	2010
			P.L. 107-16	P.L. 108-27	P.L. 108-311	P.L. 110-343	P.L. 111-5	
Threshold[b]	$75,000 HOH $110,00 MFJ	*	*	*	*	*	*	*
Phase-Out Rate	5%							
Offset AMT	NO	YES (2000-01)	YES (2002-10)	*	*	*	*	YES
Revenue Effect	-$183.38 billion	-$2.89 billion[c]	-$171.78 billion	-$32.49 billion	-$63.77 billion	-$3.13 billion	-$14.83 billion	-$91.44 billion
	(1997-07)	(2000-09)	(2001-11)	(2003-13)	(2005-14)	(2009-18)	(2009-19)	(2011-20)

Source: Joint Committee on Taxation.

Notes: *-Indicates unchanged from prior law. Except as otherwise noted, revenue effects reflect the cost of the child tax credit provisions exclusively.

[a] Prior to EGTRRA, the child credit was only refundable for families with three or more children under the alternative formula.

[b] MFS, HOH and MFJ refer to tax filing status, specifically: MFS: married filing separately; HOH: head of household; MFJ: married filing joint.

[c] This law allowed nonrefundable personal credits (including the child tax credit) to offset the regular tax in full (without regard to the tentative minimum tax) for tax year 1999 (which was an extension of a provision in P.L. 105-277). For tax years 2000 and 2001, this law included a special provision that allowed personal nonrefundable credits in full against regular tax and the AMT. The revenue effect reflects the effect of these provisions on personal nonrefundable credit, and is not limited to their effect on the child tax credit.

Before Enactment: The National Commission on Children and the Contract with America

The first child tax credit was enacted in 1997 as part of the Taxpayer Relief Act of 1997 (P.L. 105-34), but it was conceived years earlier and included in several different bills before it ultimately became law. In 1991, the bipartisan National Commission on Children,[11] which was established to provide solutions to a variety of problems facing children, recommended in its final report to the President the creation of a $1,000 refundable child tax credit for all children through age 18. Their proposed credit amount was indexed for inflation. The report cited slow wage growth, the increasing costs of living, and a rising tax burden for the average family as key factors leading to increased financial burdens on families with children.

The report's authors acknowledged that there were provisions in the tax code meant to address the increased financial burden to families that arose from having children, specifically the exemption for dependents. The dependent exemption was intended to provide economic relief to families with children by reducing taxable income by a fixed amount per dependent, and hence reducing tax liability. However, the amount of the exemption was fixed in nominal terms (i.e., not adjusted for inflation) and the commission's report highlighted the fact that its real value had declined considerably since it was established in 1948.[12] The commission argued against simply increasing the amount of the dependent exemption, noting that such a policy would not provide adequate benefit to lower- and middle-income families. Specifically, the commission noted that the dependent exemption, similar to a tax deduction, provided greater monetary benefit to taxpayers with greater taxable income since it was proportional to a taxpayer's highest marginal tax bracket. And since the dependent exemption could not lower the tax liability of taxpayers who, due to low income, owed no federal income tax, it was unavailable to many families with children who the commission believed most needed economic assistance.

Three years later, in 1994, a child tax credit was included in legislation meant to enact key principles of the Contract with America, a list of policy proposals released by the Republican Party before the 1994 midterm elections. In the 104th Congress, both the American Dream Restoration Act (H.R. 6) and later the Tax Fairness and Deficit Reduction Act of 1995 (H.R. 1215) included a $500 per child nonrefundable[13] tax credit for children under 18 years. The credit began to phase out for families with AGI above $200,000 (regardless of filing status). In response to the legislation that had been drafted in Congress, President Clinton proposed his own child tax credit during the 104th Congress in his Middle Class Bill of Rights Tax Relief Act of 1995. Under this proposal, the child tax credit was a $300 per child nonrefundable tax credit for tax years 1996 through 1998, increasing to $500 per child after 1998, with income phase-outs beginning at $60,000. The credit amounts were indexed for inflation. An eligible child was defined as being under 13 years of age.[14] President Clinton's proposal was estimated by the Treasury Department to cost $35.6 billion over five years, while the American Dream Restoration Act was estimated to cost $107 billion over the same time period.[15]

Taxpayer Relief Act of 1997 and Other Legislation

After failing to come to an agreement in 1995, Congress and President Clinton revisited the topic of a child tax credit in 1997. The House, Senate, and Clinton administration all proposed a $500 nonrefundable tax credit. A key distinction among the proposals centered on the interaction of the child tax credit with the EITC, which would have an impact on the availability of the child tax credit to lower-income taxpayers.[16] Both the Senate and House legislation proposed applying the nonrefundable child tax credit after the EITC had already reduced tax liability. President Clinton proposed the application of the child tax credit before the application of the EITC. For many low- and moderate-income taxpayers, claiming the EITC before the nonrefundable child tax credit reduced or eliminated their child tax credit. By contrast, claiming the nonrefundable child credit before the EITC allowed the taxpayer to claim the full amount of the child tax credit they were eligible for and did not change the value of their EITC. For example, assume that in 1997 a two-parent, two-child family has $23,000 of income. This family would have an $825 tax liability before the application of credits. They would also be eligible for $1,325 in the EITC and, assuming the child credit was $500 per child, $1,000 of child tax credit. If the EITC was claimed before the child tax credit, this family's tax liability would be reduced to zero and they would receive the remainder of the EITC as a $500 refund. Since they had no tax liability, they could not claim the $1,000 of nonrefundable child tax credit. If, on the other hand, they claimed the child tax credit first, they could claim $825 of the non refundable child tax credit, reducing their tax liability to zero and then claim the full $1,325 of EITC as a refund.[17]

The child tax credit proposals differed in other ways, notably the interaction of the child tax credit with the child and dependent care credit, the age of a qualifying child, and the income phase-out levels and phase-out rates. Given that the child tax credit was part of a broader tax bill that had to meet budget rules, many of the specific details of the provision were likely agreed upon after evaluating their budgetary impact.

What emerged from the conference negotiations that year was the Taxpayer Relief Act of 1997 (P.L. 105-34), which established a child tax credit. The credit was structured as a $500 nonrefundable tax credit ($400 in 1998) for most families with qualifying children under 17. The credit phased out at a rate of $50 for every $1,000 by which a taxpayer's modified AGI exceeded thresholds based on filing status, namely $110,000 for taxpayers filing as married joint, $75,000 for taxpayers filing as head of household, and $55,000 for taxpayers filing as married separate.

The credit was refundable for taxpayers with three or more qualifying children and was calculated as the excess of a taxpayer's payroll taxes over their EITC (the alternative formula). Neither the credit amount nor the phase-out thresholds were indexed for inflation. The refundable portion of the credit was reduced by the amount of the taxpayer's alternative minimum tax (AMT).[18] In addition, the total amount by which personal nonrefundable credits (including the child tax credit) could reduce an individual's regular tax liability was limited.[19]

The Omnibus Consolidated and Emergency Supplemental Appropriations Act of 1998 (P.L. 105- 277), which was enacted shortly after the enactment of the Taxpayer Relief Act of 1997, repealed the provision that reduced the refundable portion of the child tax credit by the AMT for tax year 1998. In addition, this act allowed personal nonrefundable credits (including the child tax credit) to fully offset a taxpayer's regular income tax liability in 1998.[20]

The Ticket to Work and Work Incentives Improvement Act of 1999 (P.L. 106-170) extended the provision in P.L. 105-277 which allowed the nonrefundable personal credit to fully offset regular tax liability for one additional year, through the end of 1999.

In addition, for tax years 2000 and 2001, the act included a provision which allowed taxpayers to use their personal nonrefundable credits (including the child tax credit) to not only offset their regular tax liability in full, but also their AMT. Finally, the act also extended for tax years 1999 through 2001 the prior-law repeal of the provision that reduced the refundable portion of the child tax credit by the AMT.

EGTRRA, JGTRRA, and WFTRA

The Economic Growth and Tax Relief Reconciliation Act of 2001 (EGTRRA; P.L. 107-16) made four significant changes to the child tax credit. First, EGTRRA increased the maximum amount of the credit per child in scheduled increments until it reached $1,000 per child in 2010. Second, EGTRRA made the credit refundable for families irrespective of size using the earned income formula. For tax years 2001 through 2004, the earned income formula set the amount of the refundable portion of the credit equal to 10% of a taxpayer's earned income in excess of $10,000, up to the maximum amount of the credit for that tax year. The refundability rate was scheduled to increase to 15% for tax years 2005 through 2010. The $10,000 threshold was indexed for inflation beginning in 2002. Third, EGTRRA allowed the child tax credit to offset AMT tax liability for tax years 2002 through 2010. Fourth, the law temporarily repealed the prior law provision that reduced the refundable portion of the child tax credit by the amount of the AMT. All the EGTRRA provisions were scheduled to expire at the end of 2010.

The Jobs Growth and Tax Relief Reconciliation Act of 2003 (JGTRRA; P.L. 108-27) temporarily accelerated the scheduled increase in the maximum credit amount. Specifically, while EGTRRA increased the maximum credit amount to $600 per child for 2003 and 2004, JGTRRA increased this amount to $1,000 per child for those two years. In the summer of 2003, the $400 increase in the credit for 2003 was paid in advance from the Treasury Department to many families who qualified for the child tax credit. These direct payments were distributed based on information contained on taxpayers' 2002 income tax returns. The JGTRRA provisions were scheduled to expire after 2004, and the child tax credit would have reverted to its scheduled level under EGTRRA—$700 per child in 2005.

In September 2004, Congress passed the Working Families Tax Relief Act of 2004 (WFTRA; P.L. 108-311), which further accelerated the implementation of key provisions of EGTRRA. This act extended the maximum amount of the credit established under JGTRRA, $1,000 per child, through 2009. For 2010, the EGTRRA provisions would apply and the maximum amount of the credit would remain $1,000 per child. In addition, WFTRA increased the refundability rate to 15% for 2004. Under EGTRRA, the refundability rate would remain at 15% from 2005 through 2010.

WFTRA also contained a provision that allowed combat pay to be included as part of earned income for purposes of computing refundability of the child tax credit. As more soldiers began to see combat due to the wars in

Iraq and Afghanistan, they started receiving combat pay. Income earned by members of the armed services in a combat zone is generally excluded from taxation. This exclusion benefits taxpayers who have positive tax liability and reduces the taxes they owe. However, for some lower-income members of the armed forces, the exclusion resulted in earnings being too low to qualify for the refundable portion of the child tax credit. The inclusion of combat pay as earned income for purposes of calculating the refundable child tax credit under WFTRA meant that the earnings of some military families would increase above the refundability threshold, ultimately resulting in larger child tax credit refunds. This change was for 2004 through 2010, and was scheduled to expire, along with other provisions of EGTRRA, at the end of 2010.

EESA, ARRA, and P.L. 111-312

In October 2008, Congress passed the Emergency Economic Stabilization Act of 2009 (EESA; P.L. 110-343) in response to the financial and housing crisis. The law included a provision to lower the refundability threshold for the child tax credit for 2008 from $12,050[21] to $8,500. In the absence of any additional congressional action, the refundability threshold was scheduled to increase to $12,550 in 2009.

In early 2009, Congress began to debate different legislative proposals for economic stimulus. Part of that debate concerned changing the refundability threshold of the child tax credit. The House proposed[22] reducing the refundability threshold to zero for 2009 and 2010, while the Senate proposed[23] lowering the refundability threshold to $8,100 over the same time period. The House's proposed changes to the child tax credit was estimated to cost $18.3 billion over 10 years, in comparison to $7.2 billion for the Senate proposal. The provision took its final shape during the meetings between the Senate and the House conferees.[24] In February 2009 Congress passed the American Recovery and Reinvestment Act of 2009 (ARRA; P.L. 111-5), which ultimately reduced the refundability threshold to $3,000 for 2009 and 2010. This proposal was estimated to cost $14.8 billion over 10 years.[25]

At the end of 2010, both the EGTRRA and ARRA provisions of the child tax credit (see *Table 2*) were scheduled to expire. Since ARRA's changes to the refundability threshold built upon changes made by EGTRRA, the expiration of EGTRRA would effectively terminate the expansion of refundability made by the 2009 stimulus law (ARRA). Absent an extension of EGTRRA, the maximum amount of the child tax credit would have reverted to $500 per child, the credit would only have been refundable to families with three or more children using the alternative formula, and the amount of the child tax credit would not have been allowed in full against the AMT. In December 2010, Congress passed the Tax Relief, Unemployment Insurance Reauthorization, and Job Creation Act of 2010 (P.L. 111-312), which extended both the EGTRRA provisions of the child tax credit[26] and the expansion of refundability from ARRA for two years through the end of 2012. *Table 2* summarizes the key changes made to the credit by several pieces of legislation.

Policy Considerations

The child tax credit has changed significantly since its creation in 1997, though these changes are scheduled to expire at the end of 2012. Originally the credit was nonrefundable for most taxpayers and was structured to reduce the tax liabilities of middle- and upper-middle-class families with children. While many middle-income families still benefit from this credit, more low-income families (those who have earnings above $3,000) are now also eligible for the credit.

As the expiration of the current child tax credit provisions on December 31, 2012, approaches, several policy options are available. Congress may allow the current policy to expire and the child tax credit will revert to a $500 per-child credit that is nonrefundable for most families. Congress may choose to extend current policy (both the EGTRRA and ARRA provisions), or only the EGTRRA provisions. Finally, Congress may seek to make other changes to the child tax credit. For example, Congress could change the refundability threshold, the refundability rate, the phaseout rates, and the amount of the credit per child.

Changing these parameters will affect families differently depending on their income level. These changes will also likely have significant budgetary costs. Analyzing the policy changes to the child tax credit, including extension of EGTRRA and ARRA provisions, is, however, beyond the scope of this report.

End Notes

[1] For personal taxes (for example, individual income and payroll taxes), a tax year is defined as the calendar year for which those taxes are paid. Throughout this report, the terms "tax year" and "year" will be used interchangeably.

[2] The child tax credit can be found in Section 24 of the Internal Revenue Code (26 U.S.C. § 24).

[3] With respect to the child tax credit, modified adjusted gross income (MAGI) is equal to Adjusted Gross Income (AGI) increased by foreign earned income of U.S. Citizens abroad, including income earned in Guam, American Samoa, the Northern Mariana Islands, and Puerto Rico. For more information on AGI see CRS Report RL30110, *Federal Individual Income Tax Terms: An Explanation*, by Mark P. Keightley and CRS Report RL32808, *Overview of the Federal Tax System*, by Molly F. Sherlock and Donald J. Marples.

[4] For more information on the alternative minimum tax (AMT), see CRS Report RL30149, *The Alternative Minimum Tax for Individuals*, by Steven Maguire.

[5] In the IRC, the statute refers to "social security" taxes not payroll taxes. However, "social security" taxes for the purposes of the child tax credit are defined to include both the employee's contributions to the Old-Age, Survivors, and Disability Insurance Trust Fund (6.2% of earnings) and the employee's contributions to the Hospital Insurance Trust Fund (1.45% of earnings).

[6] These figures are calculated using the 2011 formula for calculating the EITC for families with three or more children. For more information on the EITC, see CRS Report RS21352, *The Earned Income Tax Credit (EITC): Changes for 2010 and 2011*, by Christine Scott.

[7] Employee payroll taxes are calculated as 7.65% of earnings, subject to a cap, while the EITC for three or more families is calculated as 45% of earnings in the phase-in range ($0-$12,780 in 2011). Payroll taxes are greater than the EITC in the phase-out range of this credit, where the credit phases out at 21.06%.

[8] For a married couple, the EITC=0 when earnings are greater than $49,078. For single parents with more than three children, the range in 2011 is $32,275-$43,998. When earnings exceed $43,998, the EITC equals zero.

[9] For more information on what a qualifying child is for the child tax credit in comparison to other child-related tax benefits, see CRS Report RS22016, *Tax Benefits for Families: Changes in the Definition of a Child*, by Christine Scott.

[10] If the child is a non-citizen (of the U.S.), the child must be a dependent of the taxpayer, live in the U.S., and reside with the taxpayer at least half the year.

[11] For more information on the National Commission on Children, see their final report: National Commission on Children, *Beyond Rhetoric: A New American Agenda for Children and Families*, Washington, DC, 1991.

[12] In the Joint Committee on Taxation's explanation of the Taxpayer Relief Act of 1997, the committee cited the decline in the real value of the personal exemption by more than one-third over the prior 50 years as evidence of the tax system's failure to reflect a family's ability to pay. According to JCT, "The Congress believed that the individual income tax structure does not reduce tax liability by enough to reflect a family's reduced ability to pay taxes as family size increases. In part, this is because over the last 50 years the value of the dependent personal exemption has declined in real terms by over one third." For more information see U.S. Congress, Joint Committee on Taxation, JCS-23-97, *General Explanation of Tax Legislation Enacted in 1997*, December 17, 1997, pp. 6-7.

[13] The legislative language of the child tax credit included in H.R. 6 was drafted to create a new refundable credit. While the credit created by H.R. 6 could exceed a taxpayer's income tax liability, it could not exceed the sum of their income and Social Security taxes.

[14] U.S. Congress, Joint Committee on Taxation, *Background and Information Relating to Three Tax Cut Proposals for Middle Income Americans: A $500 per Child Tax Credit, A Reduction in the Marriage Penalty, and A Deduction for Education and Job Training Expenses.* 104th Cong., 1st sess., March 15, 1995, p. 5.

[15] "Treasury Release Contrasting Revenue Costs of Clinton, GOP Tax Cuts," *Tax Notes Today*, LB1290, December 16, 1994.

[16] For more information on the differences in the House, Senate and Clinton administration proposals, see Table 1 in the archived CRS Report 97-687E, *Child Tax Credits: Comparison of Proposals for Low-Income Taxpayers*, by Gregg Esenwein and Jack Taylor, available by request.

[17] All these figures are from Table 2 of the archived CRS Report 97-687E, *Child Tax Credits: Comparison of Proposals for Low-Income Taxpayers*, by Gregg Esenwein and Jack Taylor, available by request.

[18] For more information on the AMT, see CRS Report RL30149, *The Alternative Minimum Tax for Individuals*, by Steven Maguire.

[19] The total amount of personal nonrefundable credits was limited to the extent that a taxpayer's regular tax liability exceeded their tentative minimum tax. The tentative minimum tax is an alternative tax calculated using a different definition of taxable income and different tax rates. For more information on the interaction of personal tax credits and the AMT, see CRS Report RL30149, *The Alternative Minimum Tax for Individuals*, by Steven Maguire.

[20] While personal nonrefundable credits could now offset both the regular tax and tentative minimum tax, they could only offset the tentative minimum tax by an amount less than or equal to their regular tax liability. Hence these credits could not offset the AMT (which is defined as the difference between the tentative minimum and regular tax liability). For more information on the interaction of personal tax credits and the AMT, see CRS Report RL30149, *The Alternative Minimum Tax for Individuals*, by Steven Maguire.

[21] The $10,000 threshold established by EGTRRA, adjusted for inflation.

[22] H.R. 1 that passed the House on January 28, 2009

[23] S.Amdt. 570 in the nature of a substitute to H.R. 1, which passed the Senate on February 10, 2009.

[24] See the Conference Report H.Rept. 111-16.

[25] U.S. Congress, Joint Committee on Taxation, JCX-19-09, *Estimated Budget Effects Of The Revenue Provisions Contained In The Conference Agreement For H.R. 1, The "American Recovery And Reinvestment Tax Act Of 2009,"* February 12, 2009, p. 1.

[26] This includes the inclusion of combat pay as part of earned income for purposes of calculating refundability under the earned income formula created by EGTRRA. In addition this law extended for two years (through the end of 2012) the EGTRRA repeal of a prior-law provision that reduced the refundable portion of the child credit by the amount of the AMT and it extended the EGTRRA provision which allowed the child tax credit to offset a taxpayer's AMT.

In: Federal Taxes and Families ISBN: 978-1-61942-864-5
Editors: T. I. Owens and R. O. Reynolds©2012 Nova Science Publishers, Inc.

Chapter 3

THE CHILD TAX CREDIT: ECONOMIC ANALYSIS AND POLICY OPTIONS[*]

Margot L. Crandall-Hollick

SUMMARY

Certain parameters of the child tax credit are scheduled to expire in 2012 providing an opportunity to evaluate the economic impact of the current credit and examine policy options for the credit after 2012.

The child tax credit is currently structured as a $1,000-per-child credit that is partially refundable for lower-income families with more than $3,000 in earnings. Originally, the child tax credit was a $500-per-child nonrefundable tax credit which generally benefited middle- and upper-middleincome taxpayers. Legislative changes to the credit, primarily those included in the Economic Growth and Tax Relief Reconciliation Act of 2001 (EGTRRA; P.L. 107-16) and the American Recovery and Reinvestment Act (ARRA; P.L. 111-5), expanded the child tax credit's availability to some low-income taxpayers. Specifically, EGTRRA increased the maximum amount of the child tax credit from $500 per child to $1,000 per child. It also allowed lower-income taxpayers, with little or no tax liability, to claim part of the credit as a refund. ARRA reduced the refundability threshold from $10,000 (adjusted for inflation) to $3,000.These legislative changes, originally

---

[*] This is an edited, reformatted and augmented version of a Congressional Research Service publication, CRS Report for Congress R41935, from www.crs.gov, Prepared for Members and Committees of Congress ,dated July 25, 2011.

scheduled to expire at the end of 2010, were temporarily extended through the end of 2012 by the Tax Relief, Unemployment Reauthorization and Job Creation Act of 2010 ("The 2010 Tax Act"; P.L. 111-312). The child tax credit is scheduled to return to a $500 credit that is nonrefundable for most families at the end of 2012.

Two bills in the 112th Congress, the Child Tax Credit Preservation Act of 2011 (H.R. 508) and Section 105 of the Bipartisan Tax Fairness and Simplification Act of 2011 (S. 727), would permanently extend the EGTRRA provisions of the child tax credit and let the lower refundability threshold established by ARRA expire. Another option, contained in the President's FY2012 budget, would permanently extend both the EGTRRA and ARRA provisions of the credit.

To evaluate these proposals to modify the child credit, this report first provides a distributional and economic analysis of the current credit, focusing on the credit's impact on fairness or equity. The report then turns to an analysis of the current impact of the EGTRRA and ARRA modifications to the child tax credit and the potential future impact, on taxpayers with children and on the budget, of extending these provisions past 2012.

Finally, this report concludes with an overview of other possible modifications (aside from EGTRRA and ARRA provisions) to the child tax credit. The impact of these modifications will depend on a taxpayer's income. Modifications that benefit middle- and upper-middle-income taxpayers include increasing the amount of the credit per child and increasing the phase-out thresholds. Modifications that benefit lower-income taxpayers include reducing the refundability threshold or increasing the current refundability rate. These changes will likely have significant budgetary cost that policy makers may consider alongside their policy goals.

INTRODUCTION

Certain parameters of the child tax credit are scheduled to expire in 2012 providing an opportunity to evaluate the economic impact of the current credit and examine policy options for the credit after 2012. The Taxpayer Relief Act of 1997 (P.L. 105-34) created a $500-per-child nonrefundable tax credit to help ease the financial burden that families incur when they have children.[1] Since 2001, legislative changes, particularly those made by the Economic Growth and Tax Relief Reconciliation Act of 2001 (EGTRRA; P.L. 107-16) and the American Recovery and Reinvestment Act of 2009 (ARRA; P.L. 111-5), have altered the structure of this tax benefit. Specifically, the amount of the credit per child has increased and the credit has been made partially refundable, expanding the availability of the credit to some low-income families. These changes are scheduled to expire at the end of 2012, and the structure of the child tax credit will revert back to its pre-2001 form.

In light of the change to the child tax credit that is scheduled to occur at the end of 2012, the goal of this report is two-fold: (1) to analyze the economic impact of the child tax credit as it is currently structured and (2) to present policy options for changing parameters of the credit after 2012. This report first provides a brief overview of the current structure of the credit, followed by an economic and distributional analysis of the credit. The economic analysis focuses on the fairness or equity of this tax provision, based on different definitions of equity, and examines the limited impact of the credit on taxpayer behavior. The report concludes with an analysis of several policy options for the child tax credit, beginning with an in-depth examination of the extension of current policy. This report does not provide an in-depth examination of the history of the credit.[2]

CURRENT LAW

Currently, families with children may be eligible to claim a tax credit for each eligible child, subtracting the amount of the credit from their tax bill in order to reduce the taxes they owe. The current child tax credit has three key features.

- Amount: The credit equals a maximum of $1,000 per child.
- Refundability: Families with little or no income tax liability may be able to claim the credit as a refund. The amount of the refund is equal to 15% of a taxpayer's earnings above $3,000, up to the maximum amount of credit for the family. This is referred to as the "earned income" refundability formula.
- Phase-out: The credit is phased out for higher-income taxpayers. Specifically, the credit is reduced by $50 for every $1,000 a family's modified adjusted gross income (AGI)[3] exceeds specific income thresholds.[4]

The monetary parameters of the credit (credit amount, refundability threshold, and phase-out threshold) are not indexed for inflation. The child tax credit can offset a taxpayer's alternative minimum tax (AMT)[5] through the end of 2012. After 2012, the child tax credit is scheduled to revert back to its original structure. Specifically, the credit will return to a $500-per-child credit, which is nonrefundable for most taxpayers[6] and cannot offset the AMT.

WHO CLAIMS THE CHILD TAX CREDIT?

The current structure of the child tax credit benefits taxpayers over a wide range of income, as illustrated by *Table 1*. Roughly half of the child tax credit benefits goes to taxpayers with cash incomes under $50,000, whereas the other half goes to those making more than $50,000. Among taxpayers with cash income above $50,000, those with income between $50,000 and $75,000 receive the largest proportion of child tax credit benefits, 18.5%, underscoring the fact that this tax credit provides significant benefits to middle-income families. Most taxpayers with incomes above $200,000 will be ineligible for the credit due to the phase-out thresholds.[7]

Table 1. Distribution of Child Tax Credit Benefit, 2010

Cash Income[a] (2009 dollars)	Share of Total Benefit	Distribution of Tax Units[b]
Less than $10k	2.9%	10.0%
$10k to $20k	11.0%	13.5%
$20k to $30k	14.3%	12.0%
$30k to $40k	13.2%	10.3%
$40k to $50k	10.8%	7.9%
$50k to $75k	18.5%	13.3%
$75k to $100k	16.1%	11.4%
$100k to $200k	12.7%	15.8%
More than $200k	0.2%	5.4%
Total	100%	100%

Source: Tax Policy Center, Table T10-0074, February 8, 2010. Notes: Items may not sum to 100% due to rounding.

[a] Cash income includes wages and salaries, investment (taxable dividends, realized net capital gains) and business income as well as government transfer payments (social security, SSI, veterans benefits). employee contribution to tax-deferred retirement savings plans, business income or loss.

[b] A tax unit consists of an individual or married couple and their dependents that would, if their income exceeded the relevant filing threshold, file an individual income tax return.

EGTRRA and ARRA, which first made the credit partially refundable and then expanded refundability respectively, expanded the credit's availability to lower-income Americans, especially those with incomes between $10,000 and $20,000. Prior to this expansion, the credit was largely available only to middle- and upper-middle-income taxpayers. Upon expiration of the current structure of this tax benefit in 2013, many low-income Americans will be ineligible to claim the credit.

Although the current credit is available to some low-income taxpayers, very-low-income taxpayers, those with cash income of less than $10,000, receive 2.9% of child tax credit benefits, even though they make up 10% of tax units.[8] In general, taxpayers at this income level do not have any income tax liability and so cannot claim the nonrefundable portion of the child tax credit. In addition, their low income also prevents them from fully benefiting from the refundable portion of the credit. For example, a taxpayer with two children and earnings of $10,000 would be eligible for $1,050 in child tax credits, as opposed to the maximum amount of $2,000. A taxpayer with two children needs $16,333 in earnings to be able to claim the full $2,000 of child tax credit.

ECONOMIC ANALYSIS

There are a variety of ways economists evaluate tax policies, such as the child tax credit. One approach is to explore their impact on fairness or equity of the tax code. Economic theory suggests that there are two ways to analyze the fairness of a provision, vertical equity and horizontal equity. Vertical equity states that groups with more resources should pay more taxes, whereas horizontal equity states that families with the same circumstances should pay the same taxes.

Another approach is to examine how a tax provision affects taxpayer behavior, in terms of encouraging a taxpayer to do more or less of a certain activity. This is referred to as efficiency by economists. The child tax credit may have two different effects on taxpayer behavior, in terms of encouraging taxpayers to work and to have children.

Finally, economists may also choose to examine the administration and complexity of a tax provision. The administration of tax credits can affect whether tax benefits, such as the child tax credit, achieve economic or policy goals. Tax policies can thus also be analyzed with respect to their effect on the complexity of the tax code. The following section examines the child tax credit in terms of its impact on equity, taxpayer behavior, and tax administration.

Equity of the Child Tax Credit

There are several ways to assess the fairness or equity of a tax provision. Depending on the definition used, the child tax credit may or may not be equitable.

Our current income tax is progressive, meaning wealthier taxpayers pay a greater share of their income in taxes (and thus have a higher average income tax rate) than poorer taxpayers. A progressive tax system reflects a standard of fairness called vertical equity (whether taxes should be progressive and how progressive is subject to some debate).[9]

The child tax credit is generally considered vertically equitable because it reinforces the progressivity of the current income tax structure. The credit is structured to lower the tax burden of families earning between $3,000 and the phase-out income level, generally $150,000 for a married couple with two children.[10] As illustrated in *Table 2*, the child tax credit reduces the average federal tax rate of taxpayers with cash income under $200,000, while having little impact on taxpayers with income greater than $200,000. In addition, the child tax credit tends to reduce lower-income taxpayers' average tax rates more than it reduces the average tax rate of wealthier taxpayers. The largest reduction occurs among those with income between $10,000 and $20,000.

Another standard of fairness, referred to as horizontal equity, suggests that families with equal circumstances should pay equal taxes. The child tax credit's affect on horizontal equity depends on the definition of horizontal equity that is used. Some economists interpret horizontal equity to mean that families with the same amount of resources (i.e., income) should pay the same amount in taxes (and thus have the same average tax rate), regardless of whether they use those resources to buy a house, go on a vacation, or have a child. If children are viewed as choices of how taxpayers' use their resources, the credit would violate horizontal equity. Specifically, the child tax credit generally provides greater tax benefits to a family as the number of children increases, assuming their income remains unchanged.[11] For example, a married couple that has $50,000 in earnings and no children (and hence is ineligible or the child tax credit) would be expected to owe $3,800 (7.6% average tax rate) in taxes. If the same married couple had one child, they would be expected to owe $2,800 after applying the child tax credit (5.6%

average tax rate). If they had an additional child, the credit would lower their tax liability to $1,800 (3.6% average tax rate).[12]

Table 2. Federal Tax Rates With And Without The Child Tax Credit, 2010

Cash Income (2009 dollars)[b]	Average Federal Tax Rate[a]		Average Change in Federal Taxes from Credit
	No Credit	With Credit	
Less than $10k	-13.6%	-19.1%	-$347
$10k to $20k	-9.4%	-15.8%	-$994
$20k to $30k	0.5%	-5.3%	-$1,450
$30k to $40k	8.8%	4.4%	-$1,549
$40k to $50k	13.3%	9.6%	-$1,669
$50k to $75k	16.9%	14.2%	-$1,669
$75k to $100k	19.2%	17.3%	-$1,715
$100k to $200k	23.2%	22.6%	-$981
$200k to $500k	26.5%	26.5%	-$67
$500k to $1 million	26.0%	26.0%	-$60
More than $1 million	28.5%	28.5%	-$12

Source: Tax Policy Center, Table T10-0074, Feb. 8, 2010.

[a] The average federal tax rate includes individual and corporate income tax, payroll taxes and the estate tax as a percentage of average cash income. Negative tax rates indicate that taxpayers' did not owe taxes and received a refund. This may be a result of a variety of tax benefits including the standard deduction, the dependent exemption and the Earned Income Tax Credit (EITC).

[b] Cash income includes wages and salaries, investment (taxable dividends, realized net capital gains) and business income as well as government transfer payments (social security, SSI, veterans benefits), employee contribution to tax-deferred retirement savings plans, and business income or loss.

Other economists define horizontal equity to mean that families with the same "ability to pay" should pay the same in tax. Under this definition, families with more children should pay less in tax because additional children reduce their ability to pay.[13] According to the "ability to pay" approach, the child tax credit does not generally violate horizontal equity.[14] Congress used the "ability to pay" interpretation of horizontal equity to justify the structure of the child tax credit in 1997. According to the Joint Committee on Taxation, the main reason for the creation of a child tax credit was that

> Congress believed that [prior to the child tax credit] the individual income tax structure [did] not reduce tax liability by enough to reflect a family's reduced ability to pay taxes as family size increases ... The Congress believed that a tax credit for families with dependent children will reduce the individual income tax burden of those families, will better recognize the financial responsibilities of raising dependent children, and will promote family values.[15]

Policymakers may also be interested in evaluating child tax benefits like the child tax credit simultaneously with the other available tax benefits to get a holistic picture of the tax code's impact on equity. For example, as previously mentioned, the child tax credit when evaluated individually may not be horizontally equitable at low incomes. Based on this analysis, increasing refundability of the credit could make the credit more horizontally equitable for some low-income families. However, recent research suggests that after making adjustments for a family's ability to pay based on family size, the totality of child tax benefits result in a tax system that is disproportionally generous at lower income levels to larger as opposed to smaller families.[16] In this broader context, expanding refundability of the child tax credit could exacerbate horizontal inequities.

Efficiency (Behavioral Effects) of the Child Tax Credit

Economists often analyze tax provisions in terms of whether a tax provision results in more or less of a good being produced or consumed. Subsidies, which lower the prices of goods, theoretically result in more of a good being consumed and produced. The current structure of the child tax credit subsidizes both low-wage work (by the earned income formula) and children (by the $1,000 per child aspect of the provision). However, there is currently very little substantive research evaluating the impact of child tax credit on taxpayer behavior.

Impact on Work Choices

The child tax credit's current refundability structure creates a wage subsidy for some low- income families, suggesting it may affect work decisions. For eligible families with sufficiently low income, the child tax credit gives families 15 cents for every dollar of earnings above $3,000. Economic theory suggests that increasing the price of labor (the wage) among low-income workers will have the overall effect of encouraging them to work more.[17] In practice, however, it is very difficult to isolate the labor market effects of the child tax credit from the similarly structured but larger subsidy provided by the EITC, since both credits simultaneously subsidize earnings over the same income range.

Impact on Having Children

The child tax credit is unlikely to have a significant impact on inducing families to have additional children. While the child tax credit reduces the cost of a child, the expenses incurred from having children greatly exceed the value of the credit for most taxpayers. A recent government report estimates that the annual cost of raising a child in a middle-income family ranged from $11,650 to $13,530.[18] In addition, families choose to have children for a variety of factors that are not motivated by economics, including the happiness and fulfillment that children may bring them.

Complexity of the Tax Code

In a recent report to Congress, the IRS Taxpayer Advocate identified the complexity of the current tax code as the most serious problem facing taxpayers.[19] Tax policies, including those targeted towards families with children, are currently structured very differently adding to the complexity of the tax code.[20] For example, a single parent with a 16-year-old child and income of $20,000 in 2010, will be eligible for a $1,000 child tax credit, a $3,650 dependent exemption for that child (which lowers their tax liability by $548), and $2,487 of EITC. In 2011, when the child is 17, the single parent will be ineligible for the child tax credit, but remain eligible for the dependent exemption (which equals $3,700 in 2011 and will lower their tax bill by $555) and approximately $2,598 of EITC. The amount of these tax benefits will also change if the parent marries (which can change their tax liability), has an additional child, or their income changes (which changes the value of the child tax credit and EITC). Tax complexity associated with child-related tax provisions is particularly burdensome for lower-income families. Complexity reduces utilization rates among eligible populations and reduces the value of the benefits among those who do claim them, because they often rely on a paid preparer for assistance. Complexity can thus undermine the ultimate goal of policymakers, whether it be behavioral changes or increased equity.

POLICY PROPOSALS: EXTENDING EGTRRA AND ARRA

One issue facing Congress with respect to the child tax credit will be the scheduled expiration of the EGTRRA and ARRA provisions at the end of 2012. The child tax credit provisions of EGTRRA and ARRA expanded the size and availability of the child tax credit to millions of families. They also have more than tripled its annual cost. These provisions were extended through the end of 2012 by The Tax Relief, Unemployment Insurance Reauthorization, and Job Creation Act of 2010 (P.L. 111-312), henceforth referred to as the "2010 Tax Act." In order to understand the implications of extending either or both of these laws,[21] this section will examine the differing impact of the EGTRRA and ARRA modifications to the credit on taxpayers today. The analysis will then turn to the implications of extension, both on the number of children who will be affected as well as the budgetary cost.

Impact of EGTRRA and ARRA Modifications to the Credit

EGTRRA and ARRA substantially changed the structure of the child tax credit. Specifically, EGTRRA increased the value of the credit from $500 per child to $1,000 per child and made the credit partially refundable using the earned income formula. ARRA expanded upon EGTRRA's changes to refundability by lowering the earnings threshold of the earned income formula to $3,000. Collectively, these changes were scheduled to expire at the end of 2010 but where extended through the end of 2012 by the 2010 Tax Act. At the end of 2012, the child tax credit is scheduled to revert to a $500 per child credit that is nonrefundable for families with fewer than three children.

Table 3 illustrates the different impacts of the EGTRRA and ARRA provisions on taxpayers based on cash income. Overall, approximately 60% of the child tax benefits from EGTRRA went to taxpayers with cash income above $50,000. By contrast 70.5% of child tax benefits under ARRA went to taxpayers with cash income of less than $20,000.

Research suggests that the different impacts EGTRRA and ARRA have on taxpayers by income level also translate into differences by race and ethnicity. In 2005, when all the child tax credit provisions of EGTRRA were effective, 49.5% of households with qualifying African American children and 46.0% of households with qualifying Hispanic children were ineligible to receive the full credit due to low incomes, in contrast to 18.1% of households with white children.[22]

Table 3. Distribution of EGTRRA and ARRA Child Tax Credit Benefits, 2011

Cash Income (2009 dollars)	EGTRRA		ARRA		Distribution of Tax Units
	Tax Benefit (billions)	Share of Total Benefit	Tax Benefit (billions)	Share of Total Benefit	
Less than $10K	$0.1	0.2%	$1.5	18.0%	12.5%
$10K to $20K	$1.4	4.5%	$4.4	52.4%	16.5%
$20K to $30K	$4.1	13.5%	$1.9	22.7%	13.1%
$30K to $40K	$3.9	12.7%	$0.4	4.8%	10.3%
$40K to $50K	$3.0	9.9%	$0.1	1.5%	8.0%
$50K to $75K	$6.0	19.7%	$0.0	0.5%	13.1%
$75K to $100K	$6.5	21.2%	$0.0	0.2%	9.5%
$100K to $200K	$5.5	18.1%	$0.0	0.0%	11.9%
More than $200k	$0.1	0.2%	$0.0	0.0%	4.3%
Total	$29.6	100.0%	$8.3	100.0%	100.0%

Source: CRS calculations using Tax Policy Center Tables T10-0007 and T10-0005, January 12, 2010.

Notes: Items may not sum to 100% due to rounding. Tax Units includes both filing and non-filing units but excludes those that are dependents of other tax units. Tax Benefit values indicate the total value of credit in terms of reduction in revenues and increase in outlays (from the refundable portion of the credit).

Estimates of the distributional impact on tax filers of extending the EGTRRA and ARRA provisions past 2012 are currently unavailable, but can reasonably be expected to approximate the distribution in *Table 3*. Recent data do however provide information on the impact in 2013 of permanently extending these modifications in terms of the number of children who would benefit. (Although the data are presented in terms of the number of children who benefit, the tax credit is actually claimed by their parents, ostensibly for children's benefit.) These data provide another way to analyze the impact of EGTRRA and ARRA.

Extending EGTRRA and ARRA Modifications to the Credit

According to estimates provided by the Tax Policy Center, both the EGTRRA and ARRA changes to the child tax credit, if extended past 2012, would have a significant impact on the benefits received by millions of children, as illustrated in *Figure 1*.[23] In 2013, the extension of the EGTRRA provisions would result in 18.6 million children being eligible for the credit who otherwise would not receive this tax benefit if EGTRRA expired. In addition, 3.4 million children in 2013 would receive a larger credit if the EGTRRA provisions were extended.

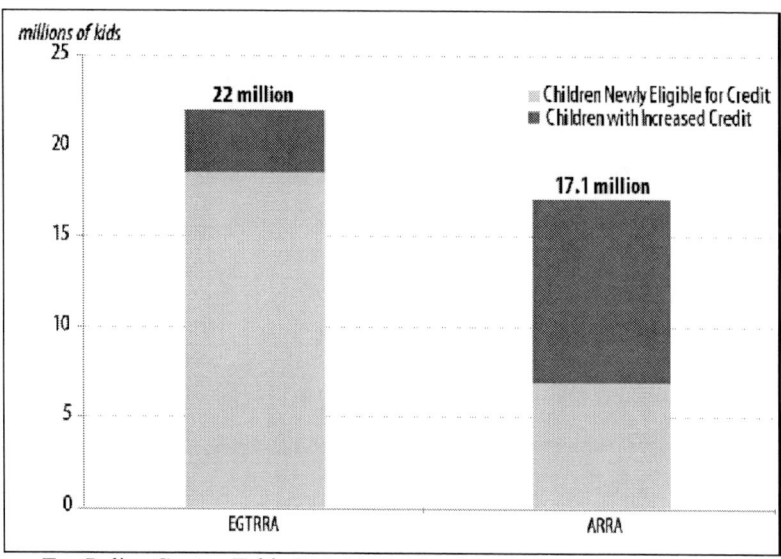

Source: Tax Policy Center, Table T11-0125, May 24, 2011.
Notes: The baseline assumes the expiration at the end of 2012 of both the EGTRRA and ARRA modifications to the child tax credit. Hence, the term "newly eligible" refers to those who are scheduled to lose the benefit entirely in 2013 under current law, but who would receive the credit in 2013 as a result of the extension of legislation. EGTRRA is the Economic Growth and Tax and Tax Relief Reconciliation Act of 2001 (P.L. 107-16) and ARRA is the American Recovery and Reinvestment Act of 2009 (P.L. 111-5).

Figure 1. Number of Children Affected by an Extension of EGTRRA and ARRA Child Tax Credit Provisions, 2013.

The extension of the ARRA modifications to EGTRRA has a lower overall benefit in terms of the impact on children. Approximately 17.1 million children would benefit from the extension of ARRA child tax credit provisions as opposed to 22 million children that benefit from the EGTRRA provisions. The majority of children who benefit from an extension of the ARRA modification would receive a larger credit (10.2 million children), while fewer would be newly eligible (6.9 million children). If EGTRRA and ARRA expired at the end of 2012, as they are currently scheduled to, an estimated 39.1 million children would either become ineligible for the child tax credit or see their child tax credit reduced in 2013.

Legislation introduced in the 112th Congress, the Child Tax Credit Preservation Act of 2011 (H.R. 508) and Section 105 of the Bipartisan Tax Fairness and Simplification Act of 2011 (S. 727), would permanently extend the EGTRRA provisions of the child tax credit and let the lower refundability threshold established by ARRA expire. Under this scenario, the credit would still be refundable for families with one or two children who had earnings above the refundability threshold, but many would see the amount of their refund fall. As the refundability threshold increases a family must have more earnings to receive the same amount of the child credit. For example, under the $8,500 threshold that applied for tax year 2008, a family with two children qualified for the full credit of $2,000 once it had earnings above $21,833. Under the $3,000 threshold set forth in ARRA, this family qualifies for the full credit when its earnings are greater than $16,333. In addition, the credit would be entirely eliminated for certain lower-income families whose earnings were between the ARRA threshold of $3,000 and the higher EGTRRA threshold which would likely exceed $12,500 by 2013.[24]

The President's FY2012 budget assumes the extension of the EGTRRA and ARRA child tax credit provisions in its baseline projection of the revenue effects of current policy.[25] In addition, the President's Fiscal Commission has proposed maintaining the child tax credit in its current form.[26]

Cost of Extending EGTRRA and ARRA Modifications to the Credit

The revenue costs associated with permanently extending the expansions to the child tax credit made by EGTRRA and ARRA are significant. The Office of Management and Budget estimates that permanently extending the EGTRRA and ARRA provisions related to the child tax credit will decrease revenues by $178.1 billion over the FY2012 to FY2021 budget window, and increase outlays (attributed to the refundable portion of the credit) by $192.8 billion over the same time period.[27] The total cost of the extension of the EGTRRA and ARRA expansions, $370.9 billion between FY2012 and FY2021, would mostly begin in 2013 and total approximately $45 billion per year in combined revenue reductions and increased spending.

Current data indicate that the majority of the cost from a permanent extension of current policy would be due to the EGTRRA provisions. The Joint Committee on Taxation's revenue estimates for the 2010 Tax Act isolate the costs of extending the EGTRRA and ARRA provisions for two years (2011 and 2012) and indicate that 78% of the cost of extending current policy results from the extension of the EGTRRA provisions. Specifically, the cost of the two-year extension of EGTRRA child tax credit provisions is $71.7 billion over 10 years (2011-2020), whereas the cost of extending the ARRA provisions is $19.7 over the same period.[28]

Of the total annual cost of the child tax credit in 2012, approximately 60% is a result of EGTRRA, 16% is a result of ARRA, and 24% is a result of the underlying parameters of the preEGTRRA credit.

POLICY OPTIONS: CHANGING OTHER PARAMETERS OF THE CREDIT

In addition to extending current policy, policymakers may consider modifying the current parameters of the child tax credit. The impact of modifications will depend on a taxpayer's income. Modifications that benefit middle- and upper-middle-income taxpayers include increasing the amount of the credit per child and increasing the phase-out thresholds. Modifications that benefit lower-income taxpayers include reducing the refundability threshold or increasing the current refundability rate. These changes will likely have significant budgetary cost that policymakers may consider alongside policy goals they may achieve by increasing this tax benefit.

Increasing the Maximum Amount of the Credit

Increasing the maximum amount of credit per child, either by a fixed amount or proportional to inflation, would be most valuable to families whose income does not exceed the phase-out limits. However, for lower-income families, those with income tax liability less than the value of their credit, increasing the maximum amount of the credit will be valuable in so far as they can claim it as refund using the earned income formula. If their earnings are sufficiently low, they may not be able to benefit from increasing the maximum amount of the credit. For example, if the child tax credit was doubled to

$2,000 per child in 2011, and all other aspects of the credit remained the same as current law, a family with two children would need earnings of at least $29,667 to claim the full credit if the maximum credit value doubled. Currently the minimum amount of earnings needed to claim the full credit for two children is $16,333.

Policymakers could also choose to increase the value of the credit by indexing it to inflation. If the $500 per child tax credit in 1998 had been indexed for inflation using the Consumer Price Index (CPI), it would be $693.14 in 2011 dollars. If the $1,000 child tax credit in effect in 2003 was indexed to the CPI it would be $1,228.07 in 2011 dollars. Increasing the amount of the credit based on inflation will not benefit certain lower-income taxpayers whose earnings tend to grow more slowly than inflation.[29]

Distribution of Benefit from Reducing the Refundability Threshold to Zero, 2011[30]	
Cash Income Level (2011 dollars)	Share of Benefit
Less than $10,000	46.0%
$10,000-$20,000	36.8%
$20,000-$30,000	11.7%
$30,000-$40,000	2.9%
More than $40,000	2.0%
Source: Tax Policy Center, Table T11-0126, May 26, 2011.	

Reducing the Refundability Earnings Threshold and Increasing the Refundability Rate

Among lower-income taxpayers, whose tax liability is less than the value of their child tax credit, the most relevant parameters of the child tax credits are those that affect refundability. Lowering the refundability threshold (currently set at $3,000) and increasing the refundability rate (currently 15%) would result in more families with low earnings being eligible to receive the credit or a larger credit. Under current law, a family with two children must earn $16,333 to be eligible to receive $2,000 in child tax credits as a refund. If the refundability threshold was lowered to zero (and all other parameters remained the same), this same family would need earnings of $13,333 to receive the full $2,000 in child tax credits as a refund. Economic modeling of this scenario indicates that roughly 95% of the benefit resulting from reducing the child tax credit refundability threshold to zero would go to taxpayers with cash income levels below $30,000. Nearly half of the benefit, 46%, would go to taxpayers with cash income below $10,000.

On the other hand, if the refundability rate was increased to 100% (meaning for every dollar a family earned above the $3,000 threshold, they received $1 of refundable credit), this same family would need earnings of $5,000 to receive the full $2,000 in child tax credits. Alternatively, if the refundability rate was the same as the refundability rate of the EITC for a family with two children (40%), this family would need earnings of $8,000 to receive the full value of the child tax credit.[32] Increasing the refundability rate and keeping the refundability threshold the same as current law would result in certain low-income households that already receive the child tax credit being eligible for a larger refundable credit. However, it would not provide any benefit to households with earnings below the refundability threshold.

Distribution of Benefit from Increasing the Refundability Rate to 40%, 2011[31]

Cash Income Level (2011 dollars)	Share of Benefit
Less than $10,000	35.2%
$10,000-$20,000	44.3%
$20,000-$30,000	14.3%
$30,000-$40,000	3.1%
More than $40,000	2.6%

Source: Tax Policy Center, Table T11-0128, May 26, 2011.

Economic modeling of a 40% refundability rate suggests that approximately 94% of the tax benefits associated with increasing the refundability rate would benefit taxpayers with cash income levels under $30,000. The greatest share of the tax benefit would go to taxpayers with cash income between $10,000 and $20,000, because their income level is significantly above the $3,000 refundability threshold such that they can benefit from the increased refundability rate.

Changing the refundable portion of the credit by changing the refundability threshold or refundability rate primarily affects lower-income families for whom the refundable portion is often the key component of the credit. Approximately 80% of the benefit that arises from reducing the refundability threshold to zero or raising the refundability rate to 40% would go to families making less than $20,000.

Increasing the Phase-out Limits of the Credit

Since the child tax credit was created in 1997, the credit has phased out for married taxpayers filing joint returns whose income[33] exceeds $110,000 ($55,000 for married couples filing separately) and for head of household filers with income above $75,000. These phase-out thresholds are not indexed for inflation. If they had been indexed for inflation, they would have been 39% higher in 2011 than they were in 1998.[34] Over the years, the real value of these thresholds has decreased due to inflation, pushing more taxpayers into the phase-out range and reducing the amount of the child tax credit these taxpayers are eligible for. One policy option would be a one-time increase in the phase-out limits. Another policy option would be indexing the amounts in accordance with established procedures applied to other elements of the tax system, such as personal exemption and the standard deduction. Finally, some combination of the two approaches is also possible.

Increasing the AGI phase-out limits for the child tax credit would significantly expand the number of taxpayers who would be eligible to receive the child tax credit. Such a change may be particularly important for taxpayers who live in areas with a high cost of living, where both incomes and costs of rearing children may be correspondingly higher. It would also increase the budgetary cost of the program. Critics of this change may question the necessity of such relief. The empirical evidence suggests that the overall federal tax burden, as well as the federal individual income tax burden, fell for most households with children between 1979 and 2007.[35] Legislation enacted since 2007 to address economic insecurity resulting from the recent recession, including ARRA and the 2010 Tax Act, have further reduced taxes for many Americans through the enactment of new provisions like the Making Work Pay tax credit (which expired at the end of 2010),[36] payroll tax reduction, and the extension of EGTRRA's individual income tax provisions.[37]

POLICY OPTIONS: REDUCING COMPLEXITY BY CREATING UNIFORM CHILD BENEFITS

Tax benefits compose a substantial proportion of the federal benefits that go to families with children. According to one study, of the five largest spending and tax programs on children, three are tax provisions—the child tax credit (number two), the EITC (number three), and the exemption for dependents (number four). Only Medicaid spending on children is higher.[38] The refundable portions of the EITC and child tax credit are structured to direct assistance to low-income families, and could reflect an increased interest by Congress to provide financial assistance to the working poor through the tax code as opposed to transfer payments. In fact, the refundable portion of the EITC and child tax credit ranked fourth and sixth respectively in outlays among programs targeted towards low-income populations.[39]

Some experts believe that the different eligibility rules for different child-related tax benefits make it increasingly difficult for taxpayers to claim these benefits. This complexity results in direct financial costs for taxpayers who may choose to use paid preparers, instead of preparing their return themselves. According to recent IRS data, more than half of taxpayers with income below $50,000 use paid tax preparers.[40] President Bush's 2005 Presidential Panel on Federal Tax Reform summarized the complexity of claiming the child tax credit, "Figuring out whether you can claim the child tax credit ... requires the skills of a professional sleuth: You need to complete eight lines on a tax form, perform up to five calculations, and fill out as many as three other forms or schedules."[41]

Much of the complexity in child related tax benefits is related to differing definitions of what constitutes an eligible child, specifically the different age limits of qualifying children among the different tax benefits.[42] The child tax credit is limited to children under 17 years old, unlike other tax benefits, like the dependent exemption that can be claimed by taxpayers with children as old as 23. Increasing the age of eligible children would have significant budgetary costs. One study estimated that expanding the child tax credit to 17 and 18 years olds would reduce revenues by $6.1 billion in 2011.[43] Beyond the differing eligibility definitions used for different child tax benefits, the tax benefits themselves are structured differently.. The interaction of these different structures has led to a middle-income families receiving a smaller total benefit than some higher-income taxpayers, as illustrated in the *Figure 2*.[44]

President Bush's 2005 Panel on Federal Tax Reform[45] recommended simplifying the tax code, including child tax benefits, but to date these proposals have not been adopted. Specifically, the panel recommended consolidating the standard deduction, personal exemption, and child tax credit into one tax benefit, a family tax credit.[46]

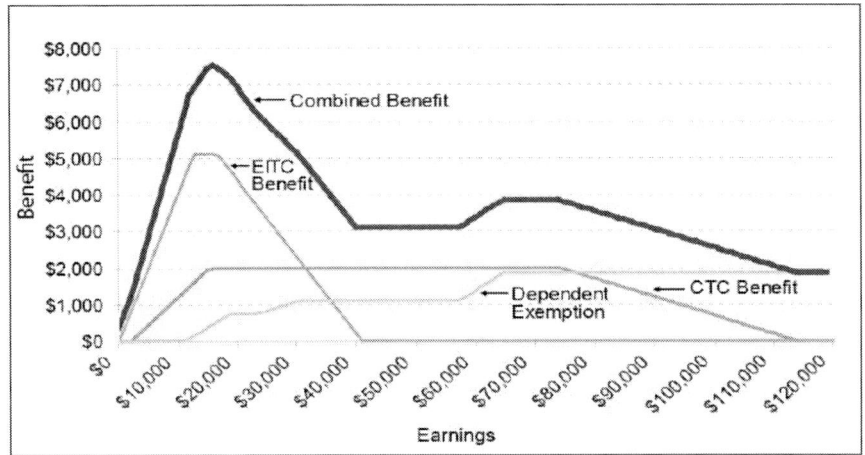

Notes: "CTC Benefit" refers to the Child Tax Credit, while "EITC benefit" refers to the Earned Income Tax Credit

Figure 2. Amount of Child Tax Benefits by Income Level, 2010 Married Couple Filing Jointly with Two Children.

More than five years later, some experts have again proposed reducing the complexity of these provisions and making their benefits more transparent by combining child tax benefits into a uniform child credit.[47] While such a proposal could significantly simplify eligibility rules as well as the calculation of the benefit, policy makers would need to consider the competing functions of current tax benefits as they create a uniform benefit. For example, some benefits like the EITC and refundable portion of the child tax credit subsidize earnings, whereas the nonrefundable portion of the child tax credit provides a uniform benefit per child for taxpayers with sufficient earnings that do not exceed the phase-out level. Because of this distinction, policymakers might consider creating different uniform credits based on the purpose of the credit, whether the purpose of the credit is to subsidize earnings of low-income taxpayers, or provide a benefit for having children.

End Notes

[1] For more information see U.S. Congress, Joint Committee on Taxation, JCS-23-97, *General Explanation of Tax Legislation Enacted in 1997*, December 17, 1997, pp. 6-7.

[2] For more information on the legislative history of the credit, see CRS Report R41873, *The Child Tax Credit: Current Law and Legislative History*, by Margot L. Crandall-Hollick.

[3] With respect to the child tax credit, modified adjusted gross income (AGI) is equal to Adjusted Gross Income (AGI) increased by foreign earned income of U.S. Citizens abroad, including income earned in Guam, American Samoa, the Northern Mariana Islands and Puerto Rico. Adjusted gross income (AGI) is equal to a taxpayer's total income minus certain adjustments to income ("above the line deductions"). AGI is the basic measure of income under the federal income tax and is the income measurement before deductions and personal exemptions are taken into account.

[4] The phase-out thresholds depend on filing status: $75,000 for single parents filing as head of household, $110,000 for married taxpayers filing jointly, and $55,000 for married taxpayers filing separately.

[5] The AMT is a parallel income tax system created by Congress to ensure that everyone pays at least a minimum of taxes and still preserves the economic and social incentives in the tax code. For more information on the AMT, see CRS Report RL30149, *The Alternative Minimum Tax for Individuals*, by Steven Maguire.

[6] After 2012, the child tax credit will still be refundable for families with three or more children using an alternative refundability formula. The alternative refundability formula is calculated as the excess of a taxpayer's payroll taxes over their Earned Income Tax Credit (EITC). For more information, see CRS Report R41873, *The Child Tax Credit: Current Law and Legislative History*, by Margot L. Crandall-Hollick.

[7] The maximum amount of income at which the credit equals zero depends on the number of eligible children for whom the taxpayer is claiming the credit. Generally $1,000 of child tax credit is reduced to zero for every $20,000 of modified AGI above the phase-out threshold. Hence, a family with five eligible children would theoretically see the child credit phase-out to zero once AGI exceeded $210,000. In addition, taxpayers with cash income above $200,000 may be able to claim the credit because modified AGI may be less than cash income in certain circumstances.

[8] The distribution of child tax credit benefits in this table reflects the distribution of the total budgetary cost (reduced revenues and increased outlays for the refundable portion of the credit).

[9] For more information on the progressivity of the tax code see CRS Report RL32693, *Distribution of the Tax Burden Across Individuals: An Overview*, by Jane G. Gravelle.

[10] In general it takes $20,000 of modified AGI to eliminate $1,000 of child tax credit. Hence, if a single parent has one child, the child tax credit will be eliminated when modified AGO exceeds $95,000.

[11] For a family with very low income and no tax liability, additional children will not necessarily increase their child tax credit and thus lower their average tax rate.

[12] In this example, the family's tax liability is arrived at by reducing their AGI (which in this case is entirely earnings) by the standard deduction and two personal exemptions for the parents to arrive at taxable income in 2011. For the two-, three-, and four-member families in this example, only two personal exemptions are applied in order to isolate the impact of the child tax credit on average tax rates. In practice, as families have children, they can also reduce their taxable income by the dependent exemption.

[13] A family's ability to pay is often calculated by making adjustments for family size that reflect that each additional family member does not increase expenses by the same amount. In other words, a family with four members does not need four times the income of a single person because the family can share certain goods like housing and utilities. For more information on approaches to calculating a family's ability to pay, see CRS Report RL33755, *Federal Income Tax Treatment of the Family*, by Jane G. Gravelle.

[14] In certain cases, primarily among certain low- and high-income families, the credit is more likely to violate this interpretation of horizontal equity. Among low-income families, the amount of the child tax credit is primarily a function of a family's earnings, not the number of children. Hence, for low-income families, the credit may not increase as the number of children does and is not horizontally equitable. For example, a family with two children and $15,000 in earnings will be able to claim $1,800 of child tax credits. If their income remains unchanged and they have an additional child, the maximum of the credit will remain $1,800. Among high-income families, the credit phases-out until it can no longer be claimed.

[15] For more information see U.S. Congress, Joint Committee on Taxation, JCS-23-97, *General Explanation of Tax Legislation Enacted in 1997*, December 17, 1997, pp. 6-7.

[16] For more information on this research, see CRS Report RL33755, *Federal Income Tax Treatment of the Family*, by Jane G. Gravelle.

[17] A wage subsidy will have two conflicting effects on the amount of labor supplied by a worker. The first effect will be to encourage the worker to work more because they are paid more ("the substitution effect"). The second effect will be to encourage the worker to work less because they can achieve the same income level with less work hours ("the income effect"). Evidence suggests that for low-income workers, the income effect is much smaller than the substitution effect, meaning a wage subsidy should increase labor-market participation for those eligible for the refundable portion of the credit. For more information on the impact of taxes and subsidies on labor supply see CRS Report RL31949, *Issues in Dynamic Revenue Estimating*, by Jane G. Gravelle.

[18] Mark Lino, *Expenditures on Children by Families, 2009.*, U.S. Department of Agriculture, Center for Nutrition Policy and Promotion., June 2010, http://www.cnpp.usda.gov/Publications/CRC/crc2009.pdf.

[19] National Taxpayer Advocate, *2010 Annual Report to Congress*, December 31, 2010.

[20] For example, child tax benefits have different phase-in and phase-out levels and eligibility requirements from the EITC and the dependent exemption. For more information on the definition of a qualifying child for different tax benefits, see CRS Report RS22016, *Tax Benefits for Families: Changes in the Definition of a Child*, by Christine Scott.

[21] Policymakers should note that the ARRA changes to the credit modified the earned income formula established by EGTRRA. In order to extend ARRA modifications, the earned income formula must also be extended.

[22] For more information see Leonard Burman and Laura Wheaton, "Who Gets the Child Tax Credit," *Tax Notes*, October 17, 2005, pp. 387-393.

[23] Data in this figure represent the number of children who would benefit from the extension of EGTRRA and ARRA child tax credit provisions in 2013.

[24] The EGTRRA threshold which was originally $10,000 in 2001, would be approximately $12,800 in 2011 due to the statutory provision to adjust the refundability threshold for inflation. Absent a deflationary period, the refundability threshold under EGTRRA would be expected to continue to increase.

[25] Department of the Treasury, *General Explanations of the Administration's Fiscal Year 2012 Revenue Proposals*, February 2011, p. 142.

[26] National Commission on Fiscal Responsibility and Reform, *The Moment of Truth*, December 2010, Figure 7, http://www.fiscalcommission.gov/sites/fiscalcommission.gov/files/documents/TheMomentofTruth12_1_2010.pdf.

[27] Office of Management and Budget, *Analytical Perspectives, Budget of the United States Government, Fiscal Year 2012: Federal Receipts*, Table 15-2, http://www.whitehouse.gov/sites/default/files/omb/budget/fy2012/assets/receipts.pdf.

[28] This includes the budgetary impact of the outlays attributed to the refundable portion of the credit.

[29] Historical data suggest that the income of lower-income Americans increases much more slowly than prices do. US Census Bureau, *Income Statistics for Families: Table F-3. Mean Income Received by Each Fifth and Top 5 Percent of Families*, http://www.census.gov/hhes/www/income/data/historical/families/index.html and Bureau of Labor Statistics, *Inflation Calculator*, http://data.bls.gov/cgi-bin/cpicalc.pl.

[30] This model assumes current law as the baseline (i.e., the 15% refundability rate, $1,000 credit per child, and $3,000 refundability threshold).

[31] This model assumes current law as the baseline (i.e., the 15% refundability rate, $1,000 credit per child, and $3,000 refundability threshold).

[32] For a family with two eligible children, increasing the refundability rate from the current level of 15% to 16% (while keeping the refundability threshold fixed at $3,000) will reduce the minimum earnings needed to qualify for $2,000 in child tax credits by $833 from $16,333 to $15,500. However, the magnitude of this effect decreases as the refundability rate increases such that when the rate is raised from 99% to 100%, the level of minimum earnings needed to qualify for $2,000 in credits falls from $5,020 to $5,000, a difference of $20.

[33] The phase-out limits are based on modified adjusted gross income (MAGI). With respect to the child tax credit, modified adjusted gross income (MAGI) is equal to adjusted gross income (AGI) increased by foreign earned income of U.S. Citizens abroad, including income earned in Guam, American Samoa, the Northern Mariana Islands, and Puerto Rico.

[34] Based on price inflation calculations using the Bureau of Labor Statistics (BLS) inflation calculator, http://www.bls.gov/data/inflation_calculator.htm.

[35] Tax Policy Center, *Historical Effective Federal Tax Rates for Households with Children*, April 8, 2011, http://www.taxpolicycenter.org/taxfacts/displayafact.cfm?Docid=459.

[36] For more information on the Making Work Pay tax credit, see CRS Report R40969, *Withholding of Income Taxes and the Making Work Pay Tax Credit*, by John J. Topoleski.

[37] The individual income tax provisions of EGTRRA reduced marginal income tax rates, reduced taxes on capital gains/dividend income, and provided marriage penalty tax relief.

[38] Julie Isaacs, C. Eugene Steurle, and Stephanie Rennane, et al., *Kids Share 2010: Report on federal expenditures on children through 2009*, Urban Institute, July 2010, Figure 3.

[39] See Table 2 in CRS Report R41625, *Federal Benefits and Services for People with Low Income: Programs, Policy, and Spending, FY2008-FY2009*, by Karen Spar.

[40] Internal Revenue Service, SOI Tax Stats., Table 2, Individual Income and Tax Data, by State and Size of Adjusted Gross Income, Tax Year 2007.

[41] The President's Advisory Panel on Federal Tax Reform, *Simple, Fair, and Pro-Growth: Proposals to Fix America's Tax System*, November 2005, p. 2.

[42] For more information on the definition of a child for child-related tax benefits, see CRS Report RS22016, *Tax Benefits for Families: Changes in the Definition of a Child*, by Christine Scott.

[43] For more information on proposals to create a uniform age for child-related tax benefits, see Elaine Maag, "Tax Simplification: Clarifying Work, Child, and Education Incentives," *Tax Notes*, March 28, 2011, pp. 1587-1596.

[44] This figure does not represent the full array of child-related tax benefits that may be available to a family. For example, it does not include the child and dependent care tax credit, or education-related tax benefits like the American Opportunity Tax Credit.

[45] The President's Advisory Panel on Federal Tax Reform, *Simple, Fair, and Pro-Growth: Proposals to Fix America's Tax System*, November 2005.

[46] Ibid, pp. 61.

[47] For more information on proposals to create a Uniform Child Credit, see Elaine Maag, "Simplicity: Considerations in Designing a Unified Child Credit," *National Tax Journal*, vol. 63, no. 4 (Part 1) (December 2010), pp. 765-780.

In: Federal Taxes and Families ISBN· 978-1-61942-864-5
Editors: T. I. Owens and R. O. Reynolds ©2012 Nova Science Publishers, Inc.

Chapter 4

DEPENDENT CARE: CURRENT TAX BENEFITS AND LEGISLATIVE ISSUES[*]

Christine Scott and Janemarie Mulvey

SUMMARY

In the 2000 census, for more than 60% of the households with children under the age of six, all parents in the household worked. Some private surveys show that nearly 40% of those caring for aging parents and older individuals worked. For families, care for young children and older individuals who are physically or mentally unable to care for themselves is critical to maintaining participation in the workforce. To assist these families, current law provides two tax benefits related to dependent care: the dependent care credit and the exclusion from income for employer-provided dependent care assistance programs. Both provisions are for employment-related expenses for the care of dependents under the age of 13, or dependents (or a spouse) who are physically or mentally incapable of caring for themselves.

Some of the current tax provisions that were expanded in 2001 are set to expire December 31, 2012. These changes include increases for the

- maximum credit rate for the dependent care tax credit (DCTC) from 30% to 35%;

---

[*] This is an edited, reformatted and augmented version of a Congressional Research Service publication, CRS Report for Congress RS21466, from www.crs.gov, Prepared for Members and Committees of Congress ,dated October 6, 2011.

- income level at which the credit rate for the DCTC phases down from $10,000 to $15,000; and
- maximum amount of qualifying expenses from $2,400 to $3,000 for one child and from $4,800 to $6,000 for two or more children.

In addition, the FY2012 Budget released by the Obama Administration in February 2011 proposes to increase the DCTC for families earning between $15,000 and $103,000 annually.

This report discusses current tax treatment of dependent care expenses under the DCTC and the dependent care assistance programs (DCAP), and issues for Congress in expanding tax benefits for working caregivers (including President Obama's Budget proposal).

INTRODUCTION

The demographics of the workforce has changed considerably in the past few decades, as has the nature of caregiving responsibilities. Not only has the share of women working increased considerably over the past three decades, but the overall workforce has aged. While many workers today still care for children, they are also increasingly more likely to be caring for aging parents.

To address dependent care costs for working caregivers, there are two current law tax provisions for dependent care: the dependent care tax credit (DCTC) and the exclusion from income for employer-provided dependent care assistance programs (DCAP). Some of the tax provisions for dependent care tax provisions are also expected to expire (not be in effect) after December 31, 2012. In addressing the expiration of these provisions, Congress may also consider whether to expand these tax incentives even more for working caregivers. The importance of this issue is underscored by the expansion of dependent care tax incentives in President Obama's Legislative Agenda[1] through the White House Middle Class Task Force chaired by Vice President Biden, which includes as one of its goals to improve work and family balance.

This report discusses

- current tax treatment of dependent care expenses under the DCTC and the DCAP, and
- issues for Congress in expanding tax benefits for working caregivers.

CURRENT TAX BENEFITS FOR DEPENDENT CARE

Under current law, there are two dependent care tax provisions targeted toward working caregivers: the DCTC is a tax credit and the DCAP is an exclusion from income for employer-provided dependent care assistance programs. These tax provisions are similar in that they both use the same definition of qualified employment-related expenses and qualifying dependent (discussed below). They differ, however, in how each affects tax liability by income category. The DCTC is a nonrefundable tax credit for qualified dependent care expenses and directly offsets tax liability dollar-for-dollar for working caregivers with a positive tax liability. The DCAP, on the other hand, is an income exclusion where the value of the tax benefit depends on a household's marginal tax rate. The DCAP is available to working caregivers whose employer offers it as a benefit. Working caregivers can only use one of these options. Both the DCTC and the DCAP rely on the same definitions of qualified employment-related expenses and qualifying dependents. This section discusses these issues in greater detail.

Qualified Employment-Related Expenses

Qualified employment-related expenses are defined by the Internal Revenue Service (IRS) as those expenses for household services and care of a qualifying dependent necessary for the taxpayer to work or to look for work. A taxpayer's work can be for others or in their own business or partnership and can be either full time or part time. Work also includes actively looking for work, but a taxpayer must have earned income to qualify in a given year.

The following are considered qualified employment-related expenses:

- Cost of care provided outside of one's home if the care is for a qualifying person who regularly spends at least 8 hours each day in his or her (i.e., taxpayer's) home.
- Care provided by a dependent care center is eligible only if the center complies with all state and local regulations.2
- Costs for transportation by a care provider to and from a dependent care center provided for a qualifying person (e.g., bus, subway, taxi, or private car) are also eligible. However, the transportation cost of

- the care provider coming to a working caregiver's home is not included.
- Fees and deposits paid to an agency to obtain the services of a care provider are included.
- Expenses paid for household services also meet the work-related expense test if they are at least partly for the well-being and protection of a qualifying person. Household services include ordinary and usual services done in and around your home that are necessary to run your home, and include services of a housekeeper, maid, or cook. However, they do not include the services of a chauffer, bartender, or gardener.

Expenses that cannot be included in this category include food, lodging, clothing, education, and entertainment. A family may pay either a private individual or a dependent care center for dependent care. A dependent care center is a facility that provides care for more than six individuals who are not residents and receives a fee or other payment for providing those services. Thus, costs of institutional care in a nursing home or assisted living facility are not included. However, payments to a dependent care center are qualified expenses only if the center meets all applicable state and local laws and regulations. However, a taxpayer can include small amounts paid for these items if they are incident to and cannot be separated from the cost of caring for the qualifying person. Qualified expenses do not include payments to a child of the taxpayer under the age of 19, or payments to an individual the taxpayer can claim as a dependent for the personal exemption.

Definition of Qualified Dependent

The Working Families Tax Relief Act of 2004 (P.L. 108-311) changed the definition of a qualifying dependent beginning in tax year 2005 to conform with changes made to the personal exemption for a more uniform definition of a child.

Qualified employment-related expenses are those expenses for household services and care of a qualifying dependent necessary for the taxpayer to be employed. For the purposes of qualified employment-related expenses, a qualifying dependent is a

- qualifying child of the taxpayer (as defined for the personal exemption) who is less than 13 years of age, and for whom the taxpayer can claim a personal exemption;
- dependent of the taxpayer who is physically or mentally incapable of providing self care, and who has lived with the taxpayer for at least half the tax year; or
- spouse of the taxpayer who is physically or mentally incapable of providing self care and who has lived with the taxpayer for at least half the tax year.

Dependent Care Credit

The DCTC is calculated as a percentage (as high as 35%) of qualified employment-related expenses for qualifying dependents.

The qualified employment-related expenses for the DCTC, beginning in tax year 2003, are actual expenses capped at $3,000 for one dependent and $6,000 for two or more dependents. If the taxpayer has two or more children, the $6,000 need not reflect $3,000 per child. The per child allocation does not matter as long as part of the $6,000 is spent on each child. The Economic Growth and Tax Relief Reconciliation Act of 2001 (EGTRRA; P.L. 107-16) raised the expense limits from $2,400 for one child and $4,800 for two or more children, and increased the credit percentage from 30% to 35%, beginning in tax year 2003. EGTRRA also increased the income level at which the credit rate begins to phase down resulting in a higher credit rate for incomes between $10,000 and $43,000. The EGTRRA increases will sunset at the end of 2012, and the DCTC will revert to tax year 2001 levels.[3]

For married taxpayers, the qualified expenses are also limited to the lesser of the taxpayer's or spouse's earned income. If the spouse is a full-time student or incapable of providing self care, they are often not employed and earning income. A special rule exists for this situation. Each month that the spouse is a full-time student or incapable of providing self care, the spouse's income for purposes of calculating the credit is assumed to be $250 for one child, and $500 for two or more children. If the spouse is a full-time student all year, this results in an income for purposes of the credit equal to qualified expense limitations of $3,000 for one child and $6,000 for two or more children.

Married taxpayers must generally file a joint return to take the DCTC, but special rules exist for couples who are legally separated or living apart. The 35% rate is reduced by 1% point for each $2,000 (or fraction thereof) by which income exceeds $15,000, but the rate is not reduced below 20%. As shown in *Table 1*, the credit is 20% at incomes above $43,000.

Table 1. Maximum Dependent Care Tax Credit by Level of Income

Adjusted Gross Income		Applicable Credit Rate	Maximum Credit Based on Number of Qualifying Individuals	
Over	But Not Over		One ($3,000 in qualified expenses)	Two or More ($6,000 in qualified expenses)
$0	$15,000	0.35	$1,050	$2,100
15,000	17,000	0.34	1,020	2,040
17,000	19,000	0.33	990	1,980
19,000	21,000	0.32	960	1,920
21,000	23,000	0.31	930	1,860
23,000	25,000	0.30	900	1,800
25,000	27,000	0.29	870	1,740
27,000	29,000	0.28	840	1,680
29,000	31,000	0.27	810	1,620
31,000	33,000	0.26	780	1,560
33,000	35,000	0.25	750	1,500
35,000	37,000	0.24	720	1,440
37,000	39,000	0.23	690	1,380
39,000	41,000	0.22	660	1,320
41,000	43,000	0.21	630	1,260
43,000	No limit	0.20	600	1,200

Source: Table prepared by the Congressional Research Service (CRS).

On the tax form, the DCTC is one of several nonrefundable tax credits[4] taken against the sum of regular and alternative minimum tax liability. In tax year 2009, a total of 6.3 million returns used the DCTC for a total credit of $3.3 billion.[5] The nonrefundable nature of the credit results in many lower-income taxpayers not being able to fully utilize the credit. For example, in tax year 2009, working caregivers with adjusted gross income (AGI) under $15,000 would not likely be able to take the DCTC because they do not have sufficient tax liability to offset with the credit. As shown in Table 2, more than 50% of DCTC is claimed by households with AGI over $50,000.

Table 2. Utilization of the DCTC by Adjusted Gross Income Tax Year 2009

Adjusted Gross Income	Percentage of Returns Claiming the DCTC	Average DCTC	Share of Total DCTC Claimed
No AGI	0.0%	$0	0.0%
$1 up to $15,000	0.0%	$156	0.1%
$15,000 up to $25,000	2.6%	$365	6.1%
$25,000 up to $40,000	4.9%	$603	20.7%
$40,000 up to $50,000	5.2%	$530	9.0%
$50,000 up to $75,000	6.5%	$512	18.7%
$75,000 up to $100,000	9.1%	$533	16.8%
$100,000 up to $200,000	10.6%	$542	23.5%
$200,000+	8.1%	$532	5.1%
All Taxpayers	4.5%	$528	100.0%

Source: Table prepared by CRS using data from IRS Data from Individual Complete Report (Publication 1304).

Employer-Provided Dependent Care Assistance Programs

A taxpayer can exclude from income up to $5,000 paid or incurred by an employer for qualified dependent care expenses under an employer-provided DCAP. The DCAP definitions for qualified dependent care expenses and qualified dependent are the same definitions as for the DCTC. An employer can provide direct payment to child care and adult day care providers, provide on-site child care, or reimburse parents for child care they obtain. Similar to the DCTC, payments made to a dependent of the taxpayer or a child of the taxpayer under the age of 19 are not excluded from income.

These arrangements are often funded through salary reduction agreements. Under a salary reduction agreement, the employee agrees that a specified amount be set aside for the employer's DCAP.[6] The employer DCAP must be a written plan meeting certain rules for nondiscrimination among employees, but need not be funded by the employer. By using a salary reduction, an employee receives the benefit of the income exclusion during the tax year rather than at year's end.

The tax benefit from a DCAP depends on the marginal tax rate of the working caregiver and the amount that the working caregiver allocates to the DCAP each year. The marginal tax rate is defined as the tax rate on the last dollar that the person earned that year and increases with income. Higher tax benefits from the DCAP accrue to individuals with higher marginal tax rates. Although the working caregiver also does not pay employment taxes (i.e., Social Security and Medicare payroll taxes) on the amount he or she contributes to the DCAP, these taxes generally do not vary by income.[7] Thus, higher-income individuals receive a higher DCAP tax benefit than middle- and lower-income individuals.

According to a Mercer survey, 24% of small employers (10 to 499 employees) and 83% of large employers (500+ employees) offered a DCAP to their employees in 2009. The average contribution to a DCAP was about $3,050, which is lower than the $5,000 maximum allowed under current law.[8] This difference may reflect the "use or lose" nature of the funds and changes in employment (for example, if an employee changes jobs from one employer who offers a DCAP to another who does not).[9] Funds for dependent care expenses not used by the end of the year revert back to the employer.[10] The Mercer survey found that an average of 1% of funds are forfeited under the use or lose rules.

Interaction Between the DCTC and the DCAP

Although both provisions use the same definition of employment-related expenses, the same expenses cannot be used for both the DCTC and DCAP. Taxpayers must choose between the two tax provisions for the same qualified dependent care expenses. For taxpayers in tax brackets higher than the DCTC credit rate, the DCAP using a salary reduction arrangement is more advantageous. However, because the DCTC has a higher limit ($6,000) in the case of two or more children, a higher-income taxpayer may use up to $5,000 in a DCAP with a salary reduction, and use $1,000 of taxpayer paid employment-related expenses for the DCTC.

ISSUES FOR CONGRESS

A key issue Congress may consider is expiring provisions relating to the maximum credit rate, the maximum amount of the qualifying expenses, as well as other provisions relating to the integration of the dependent care tax credit with other areas of the tax code (such as EITC and AMT). In doing this, Congress may also look at whether these provisions are adequately addressing the costs for working caregivers. This issue is also at the forefront of President Obama and Vice President Biden's Initiatives for Middle-Class Families. Included in their blueprint is a proposal to double the child and dependent care tax credit.

In addition to addressing the expiration of a number of provisions, some areas Congress may look at for expansion include the following:

- the definition of dependent to include care recipient populations that are not otherwise included under current law.
- the amount of work-related expenses that are used for calculating the DCTC or DCAP formula.
- the benefit to allow more lower-income caregivers to participate. The following includes greater detail on each of these options.

Expiring Provisions

A number of provisions for dependent care are set to expire (not be in effect) after December 31, 2012.[11] Initially provisions authorized by the Economic Growth and Tax Relief Reconciliation Act of 2001 (EGTRRA; P.L. 107-16) were set to expire on December 31, 2010, but they were recently extended to December 31, 2012, through the Tax Relief Unemployment Insurance Reauthorization, and Job Creation Act of 2010 (P.L. 111-312). Changes that are set to expire include the increases for the

- maximum credit rate for the DCTC from 30% to 35%;
- income level at which the credit rate for the DCTC phases down from $10,000 to $15,000; and
- maximum amount of qualifying expenses from $2,400 to $3,000 for one child and from $4,800 to $6,000 for two or more children.

Expand Definition of Care Recipient

One area for expansion relates to the definition of dependent who is the care recipient. Specifically, there has been interest to expand the definition to include aging parents or relatives or other care recipients who may not be living with the care provider.

As noted earlier, one key requirement for a dependent to be covered is that the care recipient must be physically or mentally incapable of caring for himself or herself, and he or she must live with the working caregiver for more than half the year. One of the key issues in expanding the definition of "dependent" is that the second criterion that requires the expenses to be work-related would still have to be met. It may be difficult to prove that expenses for someone currently not living with a working caregiver meet this IRS criteria discussed earlier.

Increase the Amount of Work-Related Expenses that Are Deductible or Credited

Neither the DCTC or DCAP maximum allowable amounts have been indexed for inflation, and survey data indicate that dependent care cost may far exceed existing thresholds. A recent survey from the National Association of Child Care Resource and Referral Agencies found that the average annual cost of care for an infant in a center in 2010 ranged from more than $4,650 in Mississippi to more than $18,200 in the District of Columbia. For a four-year-old, the average cost of care ranged from more than $3,900 in Mississippi to more than $14,050 in the District of Columbia in 2010. Parents of school-age children paid more than $2,450 in Louisiana and Tennessee to more than $10,400 in New York.[12] Among older care recipients, eldercare costs are also expensive. According to a recent survey, the median annual cost of adult day care is $15,600.[13] Thus, the current amount of work-related expenses that are allowed as a deduction through a DCAP of $5,000 or taken as a tax credit through the DCTC (from $3,000 to $6,000 depending on number of children) may not be sufficient to adequately cover eligible expenses for working caregivers.

To increase the amount of the work-related expenses that are subject to either a deduction or a credit, one direct approach is to increase the maximum thresholds for both the DCTC and the DCAP.

Another way to indirectly affect the amount of the available credit under the DCTC is to modify the applicable credit rate or the income thresholds. Under current law, the amount of the work-related expenses eligible for the credit depends on a taxpayer's adjusted gross income. Lower-income individuals are permitted to take a higher share of expenses than higher-income taxpayers. Changing the applicable credit rate can increase the availability of the credit to middle-income households.

This later approach was proposed by President Obama in his FY2012 Budget, which proposes to increase the credit for families earning between $15,000 and $103,000 annually. Specifically, the Budget proposes to permanently increase from $15,000 to $75,000 the adjusted gross income level at which the credit begins to phase down, maintaining the percentage point phase down for every $2,000 (or part thereof) in additional income, until the rate reaches 20% for taxpayers with incomes over $103,000.[14] The Budget proposes to make this provision effective for taxable years beginning after December 31, 2011, meaning that the results of increasing the credit would likely not be seen until FY2013. *Table 3* shows the impact of the President Obama's proposal on the amount of the dependent care expenses that would be eligible for the credit.

Expand the Credit to Allow More Lower-Income Caregivers to Participate

A key concern of the DCTC is the inability of lower-income households to take advantage of the credit because the credit is nonrefundable. As noted earlier, a nonrefundable credit cannot be used in full if a working caregiver's tax liability is less than the amount of the credit. One legislative option is to make the credit refundable.

Lower-income households would benefit the most from making the tax credit refundable. As shown in earlier in *Table 2*, very few households with AGI up to $15,000 are eligible under current law for the DCTC because they have no tax liability. Those taxpayers with AGI of between $15,000 to

$25,000 would only be eligible for part of the DCTC because they would not have sufficient tax liability to offset the full DCTC amount. Under current law, 60% of the tax benefits from the DCTC accrue to taxpayers with AGI over $50,000.

Estimates by the Tax Policy Center show that if the DCTC had been fully refundable in 2006, an additional 1.6 million households would have claimed the credit and the cost of the credit (in lost revenues) would have increased by $1.7 billion.[15]

Table 3. Maximum Dependent Care Tax Credit Under Obama FY2012 Budget Proposal

Adjusted Gross Income		Applicable Credit Rate	Maximum Credit Based on Number of Qualifying Individuals	
Over	But Not Over		One ($3,000 in qualified expenses)	Two or More ($6,000 in qualified expenses)
$0	$75,000	0.35	$1,050	$2,100
75,000	77,000	0.34	1,020	2,040
77,000	79,000	0.33	990	1,980
79,000	81,000	0.32	960	1,920
81,000	83,000	0.31	930	1,860
83,000	85,000	0.30	900	1,800
85,000	87,000	0.29	870	1,740
87,000	89,000	0.28	840	1,680
89,000	91,000	0.27	810	1,620
91,000	93,000	0.26	780	1,560
93,000	95,000	0.25	750	1,500
95,000	97,000	0.24	720	1,440
97,000	99,000	0.23	690	1,380
99,000	101,000	0.22	660	1,320
101,000	103,000	0.21	630	1,260
103,000	No limit	0.20	600	1,200

Source: CRS Estimates.

End Notes

[1] See http://www.whitehouse.gov/sites/default/files/Fact_Sheet-Middle_Class_Task_Force.pdf.

[2] A dependent care center is a place that provides care for more than six person and receives a fee, payment, or grant for providing services of any of those persons, even if the center is not run for profit.

[3] These provisions were initially scheduled to expire December 31, 2010, and were extended to December 31, 2012, by the Tax Relief, Unemployment Insurance Reauthorization, and Job Creation Act of 2010 (P.L. 111-312).

[4] Other nonrefundable credits include those for education, retirement savings, adoption, and the child credit (which is refundable for certain taxpayers).

[5] Internal Revenue Service, *Individual Complete Report (Publication 1304)*, Table 3.3, available at http://www.irs.gov/pub/irs-soi/09in33ar.xls.

[6] The plan will then reimburse the employee from the set aside amount (employee contributions) for dependent care expenses. This type of arrangement is also known as a flexible spending arrangement or flexible spending account, and is often offered as part of a cafeteria benefit plan, in which employees may choose from one or more taxable or nontaxable benefits.

[7] The one exception is for workers whose wages exceed the maximum amount subject to the Social Security payroll tax in which case there is no Social Security payroll tax savings.

[8] Mercer Human Resource Consulting, National Survey of Employer Sponsored Health Plans, released July 2010.

[9] Employers at their discretion may extend the deadline for using unspent balances up to 2½ months after the end of the plan year.

[10] See CRS Report RL32656, *Health Care Flexible Spending Accounts*, by Janemarie Mulvey.

[11] The Economic Growth and Tax Relief Reconciliation Act of 2001 (EGTRRA; P.L. 107-16) provisions were set to expire on December 31, 2010, and the Tax Relief Unemployment Insurance Reauthorization, and Job Creation Act of 2010 (P.L. 111-312) extended these provisions in EGTRRA to December 31, 2012.

[12] National Association of Child Care Resource and Referral Agencies, *Parents and the High Price of Child Care: 2011 Update*.

[13] Genworth Financial, *2011 Cost of Care Survey: Home Care Providers, Adult Day Care, Health Care Facilities, Assisted Living Facilities and Nursing Homes*, April 28, 2011.

[14] U.S. Department of the Treasury, *General Explanations of the Administration's FY2012 Revenue Proposals*, p. 4, http://www.treasury.gov/resource-center/tax-policy/Documents/Final%20Greenbook%20Feb%202012.pdf.

[15] Roberton Williams, *President-Elect Obama's Tax and Stimulus Plans*, Tax Policy Center, January 2009. See also, Jeffrey Rohaly, *Reforming the Child and Dependent Care Tax Credit*, Tax Policy Center, May 30, 2007, The Urban Institute and Brookings Institution.

In: Federal Taxes and Families ISBN: 978-1-61942-864-5
Editors: T. I. Owens and R. O. Reynolds ©2012 Nova Science Publishers, Inc.

Chapter 5

TAX BENEFITS FOR FAMILIES: ADOPTION[*]

Christine Scott

SUMMARY

The federal government provides assistance for the adoption of children through federal grants to states and through the tax code. Although federal assistance programs for adoption focus primarily on children adopted out of foster care, federal adoption tax provisions are available for all adoptions (except for adoptions of stepchildren).

Congress created federal tax assistance for adoption by enacting the Small Business and Job Protection Act of 1996 (P.L. 104-188). The act added tax incentives for adoption to the existing federal adoption assistance grant programs by creating a tax credit and an income tax exclusion of up to $5,000 per adoption and $6,000 per adoption of a special needs child. The Economic Growth and Tax Relief Reconciliation Act of 2001 (EGTRRA, P.L. 107-16) increased qualified expenses for the credit (and the income tax exclusion) to $10,000 (indexed for inflation), but with a sunset period.

The Patient Protection and Affordable Care Act (P.L. 111-148) provided, for tax years 2010 and 2011 only, that the adoption tax credit

---

[*] This is an edited, reformatted and augmented version of a Congressional Research Service publication, CRS Report for Congress RL33633, from www.crs.gov, Prepared for Members and Committees of Congress ,dated July 22, 2011.

be refundable. P.L. 111-148 also increased the qualified expenses for the adoption tax credit and the income tax exclusion for employer provided adoption assistance to $13,170 for tax year 2010, with this amount indexed for inflation in 2011.

The Tax Relief, Unemployment Insurance Reauthorization, and Job Creation Act of 2010 (P.L. 111-312) extended the EGTRRA provisions for adoption to tax year 2012. Beginning in tax year 2013, pre-EGTRRA law will be effective—a $6,000 limitation and applicable for special needs adoptions only, no income exclusion for employer provided adoption assistance, and the adoption tax credit will be nonrefundable.

The tax credit and the income tax exclusion significantly limit who may benefit from the tax provisions. Both provisions are subject to a phase-out rule (which creates an income cap). These provisions, combined with the nonrefundability of the credit in prior years, limited the number of taxpayers who benefited from the credit. As a result, in tax year 2008, very few families with an adjusted gross income of less than $30,000, or with an adjusted gross income of $200,000 or more, claimed the credit. In tax year 2008, approximately 86,600 tax returns, or .06% of all tax returns, included a claim for the adoption tax credit, with a total credit value claimed of $353.5 million.

Policy issues associated with the tax provisions are the limited availability of the credit resulting from the phase-out rule, more generous provisions for domestic adoptions and for adoptions of special needs children, and whether the tax system is the most efficient means of providing federal assistance for adoption.

This report outlines the tax benefits for adoption, examines the associated policy issues, and provides a legislative history of the tax provisions for adoption.

INTRODUCTION

States have paramount responsibility in setting policy to govern the process of child adoption. Nonetheless, the federal government plays a significant—though indirect—role in supporting adoption through grants to states that provide both one-time and ongoing subsidies to parents of adoptive children with special needs and through tax benefits that help offset the costs of adopting a child. This report focuses primarily on the latter—the federal adoption tax credit and income tax exclusion for employer-provided adoption assistance.

SCOPE OF ADOPTION

There are several types of adoption, including domestic public agency adoption, domestic private adoption, and intercountry adoption. With regard to each of these types of adoption, the Department of Health and Human Services (HHS) collects data on children adopted with the involvement of state child welfare agencies, and the Department of State records the number of intercountry adoptions through its visa reporting system. However, statistics on private adoptions are the least reliable or consistent, because private agencies and individuals who facilitate independent adoptions are not required to report data to either state or federal agencies.

The most recent data on all types of adoption, collected by the National Center for State Courts (NCSC), indicate than an estimated 127,000 children were adopted in 2001.[1] According to NCSC data, of adoptions in 2001, an estimated 46% were private (including tribal and kinship, such as stepparent), 39% were intercountry, and 15% were public agency adoptions.

The tax provisions described in this report cover all types of adoption, except for adoptions by stepparents. According to data for 1992 (the most recent available), the majority of private adoptions (or 42% of total adoptions) were by stepparents.[2]

Domestic Public Agency Adoptions

Children in state foster care are typically placed in either foster family homes, relative foster homes, group homes, or institutional settings such as hospitals or residential treatment centers. On the last day of FY2009, approximately 424,000 children were in foster care[3] and 115,000 were "waiting" to be adopted.[4] (Foster children waiting to be adopted include those who have a permanency goal of adoption or those whose parental rights have been terminated.) During FY2009, approximately 57,500 children were adopted with the involvement of state child welfare agencies.[5]

Domestic Private Adoptions

Domestic private adoptions are facilitated by state-licensed private agencies or through independent agreements in which an individual arranges for another party to adopt his or her child.[6] Like all adoptions, private adoptions are finalized by state or tribal courts, but data on these adoptions are not systematically collected or reported. Therefore, national data on domestic private adoptions are the least reliable or consistent. The most recent effort to count domestic private adoptions was in 2001 when, as noted earlier, the National Center on State Courts estimated them at 58,600 (or 46% of the estimated 127,000 adoptions of all kinds) adoptions.

Intercountry Adoptions

Intercountry (also called foreign or international) adoptions are adoptions of non-citizen or resident children by families who are citizens or legal residents of the United States.[7]

In FY2010, the Department of State reports that there were 11,059 incoming (from other countries) adoptions.[8]

OVERVIEW OF THE TAX CREDIT AND INCOME TAX EXCLUSION

Adoption costs can exceed $40,000, depending on the type of adoption, with the following ranges:[9]

- Domestic public agency adoptions: $0 to $2,500.
- Domestic private adoptions: $5,000 to $40,000 (or more).
- Intercountry adoptions: $15,000 to $30,000 (or more).

The federal adoption tax credit and income tax exclusion (for employer-provided adoption expenses) are intended to help offset some of the costs of adoption for taxpayers.[10]

Both the credit and the income tax exclusion are subject to the same phaseout (or income limitation) and the same maximum qualified expenses that can be claimed per adoption.

Both tax provisions use the same definitions of qualified expenses, eligible child and special needs child, and both have the same special rules for intercountry adoptions.

The Adoption Tax Credit

The Adoption Tax Credit is available to taxpayers who have either initiated or completed the adoption process.[11] Unlike many other tax credits, the adoption tax credit has a 100% credit rate—the amount of the credit is the same as the amount of qualified expenses. The dollar limit for qualified expenses is adjusted annually for inflation.[12] In tax year 2011, the dollar limit for qualified expenses is $13,360.

The most recent public data available on the use of the adoption tax credit by the type of adoption are for tax year 2004. In tax year 2004, taxpayers claimed adoption tax benefits for the adoption of 12,432 children with special needs, or about 18% of all adoptions for which tax benefits were claimed. In contrast, in that same year, taxpayers adopting internationally claimed some part of the tax credit for 29,296 adoptions, representing about 33.7% of the adoptions for which tax benefits were claimed.[13] In contrast, in tax year 1998, tax benefits were claimed for the adoption of 50,400 individuals including 4,700 special needs children, and 14,300 intercounty adoptions. Although the total number of adoptions for which tax benefits are claimed has increased, the growth for special needs children is significant.

Qualifying Expenses

A taxpayer can claim only expenses that are necessary and reasonable and directly related to the adoption of an eligible child.[14] The term "eligible child" refers to children under age 18 and to individuals who are physically or mentally incapable of taking care of themselves.[15] Qualified expenses do not include those that violate federal or state law, are incurred in carrying out any surrogate parenting agreement, or are for the adoption of a child who is the child of the taxpayer's spouse (i.e., a stepchild).[16]

For domestic adoptions, taxpayers may claim the adoption tax credit in the tax year following the tax year that they incur the qualifying expense, without regard to the status of the adoption. This means that even if an adoption is never finalized, the taxpayer may claim the adoption tax credit for the qualified expenses associated with the adoption. For intercountry adoptions, the adoption must be finalized before the taxpayer can claim the adoption tax credit for any qualifying expenses. Specific types of expenses eligible for the credit are not listed in the Internal Revenue Code (IRC). Table 1 shows examples of qualified expenses provided by Internal Revenue Service (IRS) publications.

Table 1. Examples of Qualifying and Non-Qualifying Expenses

Qualifying Expenses	Non-Qualifying Expenses
—court costs —attorney fees —adoption fees —travel expenses —re-adoption expenses in the case of intercountry (foreign) adoptions —other costs directly related to the adoption	—expenses already covered by assistance through state, federal, employer or other programs —expenses that violate state or federal law —expenses incurred for an adoption carried by a surrogate —expenses incurred for adopting a spouse's child —expenses paid before 1997

Source: Internal Revenue Service, Instructions for Form 8839.

Note: These lists are not exhaustive but are intended to illustrate what are considered qualifying expenses and non-qualifying expenses.

Special Rules for Special Needs Children

Beginning with tax year 2003,[17] a taxpayer claiming the credit for the adoption of a special needs child is assumed to have incurred the maximum amount of qualifying expenses and may claim the full credit.[18] Many children adopted from the public child welfare system meet the definition of special needs for the adoption tax credit. A child is defined as a special needs child if the child's state of residence determines that

- the child cannot, or should not, be returned to the home of his or her birth parents;
- there is a specific factor or condition which leads to the reasonable conclusion that the child will not be adopted without assistance provided to the adoptive parents;
- and the child is a citizen or legal resident of the United States.

Examples of specific factors (or conditions) that may be considered in determining whether a child is a special needs child include ethnicity; minority status; age; status as part of a sibling group; mental, emotional or physical handicap; and other medical conditions.[19] The definition of "special needs" for the adoption tax credit matches the definition provided in Section 473 (Title IV-E) of the Social Security Act for the federal Adoption Assistance Program.

Special Rules for Intercountry Adoptions

For purposes of the tax code, a child must be a legal resident or citizen to qualify as a special needs child; therefore, no intercountry adoption meets the tax code's definition of special needs.[20] Although a taxpayer may not claim a total adoption tax credit of more than $13,360 in tax year 2011 for any single adoption, the taxpayer may claim the adoption tax credit for a single adoption in more than one tax year, depending on when the adoption expenses are paid and whether the adoption is domestic or intercountry. For a domestic adoption, the qualifying expenses may be claimed for the adoption tax credit prior to and during the adoption process, even if the adoption is not finalized; for an intercountry adoption, the adoption *must* be finalized before a taxpayer can claim the credit for the adoption expenses.[21] Therefore, a taxpayer adopting a foreign child may only claim the credit beginning in the tax year in which the adoption is finalized. *Table 2* shows the relationship between the tax year in which expenses are paid and the tax year when those expenses are eligible for the adoption tax credit, based on the type of adoption.

Table 2. When Qualified Expenses Are Eligible: Domestic and Intercountry Adoptions

When the Qualified Expenses Are Incurred	When Taxpayer May Claim Expenses	
	Domestic Adoptions	Intercountry Adoptions
Tax years before the tax year in which the adoption is finalized	Tax year following the tax year in which expenses are incurred (or later tax years)	Tax year in which the adoption is finalized (or later tax years)
Tax year in which the adoption is finalized	Tax year in which the adoption is finalized (or later tax years)	Tax year in which the adoption is finalized (or later tax years)
Tax years after the tax year in which the adoption is finalized	Tax year in which expenses are incurred (or later tax years)	Tax year in which expenses are incurred (or later tax years)

Source: IRS, Instructions for Form 8839.

Limitations

In addition to the maximum amount for qualified expenses, one other significant limitation is related to the credit. The first is the phase out of the credit, or maximum income limitation. The full credit can only be claimed by families with an adjusted gross income (AGI)[22] equal to or less than $185,210 in tax year 2011.[23] For taxpayers with incomes above this threshold amount, their credit is reduced by the ratio of their income above the threshold to $40,000. For example, a taxpayer with an AGI of $190,000 would have their credit reduced by 12.0% (calculated as $190,000 - $185,210, or $4,790 divided by $40,000, equals 12.0%). For taxpayers with an AGI $40,000 or more above the threshold,[24] the credit is reduced to zero ($0).

Claiming the Credit

To claim the adoption tax credit, a taxpayer must fill out IRS Form 8839. Depending on the taxpayer's marital status, the filing requirements may vary. Generally, a married couple must file a joint tax return to claim the adoption tax credit.[25] If two taxpayers (not married to each other) wish to claim the adoption tax credit, they may split the qualified expenses for the adoption tax credit (and therefore the adoption tax credit) by mutual agreement.[26] However, the total of qualified expenses (and adoption tax credit) cannot exceed the maximum allowed under law ($13,360 in tax year 2011). Taxpayers must include the tax identification number (Social Security number) of the child they are adopting.[27] Finally, taxpayers must keep all receipts and records of expenses for reporting purposes.[28]

Income Tax Exclusion for Employer Adoption Assistance

Generally, the income tax exclusion for employer adoption assistance follows many of the same rules, applications, and limitations as the adoption tax credit.[29] The maximum amount of qualified expenses that can be claimed is subject to the same dollar limitation as the tax credit.[30] A taxpayer's eligibility for the income tax exclusion is also subject to the same income limitation (or phaseout) as the adoption credit.[31] The income tax exclusion for employer-provided adoption assistance follows the same definitions of special needs children, qualified expenses, and eligible children. The special rules for intercountry adoptions and filing requirements of the adoption tax credit also apply to the income tax exclusion.[32] Individuals can use both the adoption tax credit and the income tax exclusion (if both are available to them), but cannot claim the same expenses for both tax provisions.[33] Employer-provided adoption assistance must be provided through a separate written plan for an adoption assistance program, which is generally available to all employees. However, employers are restricted from offering the adoption assistance program to certain high-earning employees.[34]

Unlike the adoption tax credit, employer adoption assistance programs act as income tax exclusions. This means that an employee who has qualifying expenses covered through an employer adoption assistance program (expenses paid for by the employer or through a reimbursement program funded by the employer, employee, or both parties) does not have to include the value of the covered adoption expenses as income for federal income taxes.[35] Employer adoption assistance programs are a separate employee benefit and are provided by direct payment of eligible expenses by the employer or the reimbursement of eligible expenses through an account (usually administered by a third party) funded by the employee, employer, or both.[36] Employers may include an adoption assistance program based on reimbursement as part of a cafeteria plan for employee benefits, and reduce an employee's salary to pay for the benefit. Companies may offer informational and referral benefits, direct payment or reimbursement of eligible expenses, paid leave benefits, or a combination of benefits for adoption.[37]

According to the Department of Health and Human Services, a Hewitt Associates study found that 39% of major U.S. companies offered adoption assistance as an employee benefit.[38] Employers sampled by Hewitt offered from $1,500 to $15,000, with an average of $3,879 in reimbursement of adoption expenses.[39] Because an employer has discretion in the amount and type of assistance offered for adoption, the income tax exclusion for employer-provided adoption assistance may be more limited than the adoption tax credit in the types of eligible adoption assistance.

Although employer-provided adoption assistance is excluded from federal income taxes, unlike other flexible benefits such as child care, *it is still subject to Social Security and Medicare taxes.*

POLICY ISSUES

Several policy issues are associated with the federal adoption tax provisions, including the limitation on the credit (the phaseout), the rules for special needs children and intercountry adoptions, the sunset of the EGTRRA changes, and whether the tax provisions are the best way to provide adoption assistance.

Phaseout (Income Limitation)

As noted earlier, the full credit can only be claimed by families with an adjusted gross income (AGI)[40] equal to or less than $185,210 in tax year 2011.[41] For taxpayers with incomes above this threshold amount, their credit is reduced by the ratio of their income above the threshold to $40,000. For example, a taxpayer with an AGI of $190,000 would have their credit reduced by 12.0% (calculated as $190,000 - $185,210, or $4,790 divided by $40,000, equals 12.0%). For taxpayers with an AGI $40,000 or more above the threshold,[42] the credit is reduced to zero ($0).

As shown in *Table 3*, taxpayers claiming the adoption tax credit in tax year 2008 accounted for only .06% of all tax returns, reflecting a relatively small number of all taxpayers claiming the adoption tax credit. Few taxpayers claiming the adoption tax credit had an AGI of less than $30,000 or more than $200,000. As shown in *Table 3*, the average credit for every AGI class was below the maximum adoption tax credit. However, the average credit increases with the AGI class, reflecting the increase in tax liability to offset with the credit, as prior to tax year 2010, the tax credit was nonrefundable. The exception is the $200,000 or more AGI class in which few taxpayers claim the adoption tax credit, reflecting the phaseout of the adoption tax credit.

Table 3. Utilization of the Adoption Tax Credit, Tax Year 2008

Adjusted Gross Income Class	Total Tax Returns	Tax Returns with the Adoption Tax Credit	Share of Total Tax Returns	Amount of Adoption Tax Credit	Average Credit Amount per Return
Under $30,000	67,656,220	3,030	0.00%	$1,054,000	$348
$30,000 to under $50,000	25,641,403	20,568	0.08%	$23,234,000	$1,130
$50,000 to under $75,000	19,196,461	23,610	0.12%	$75,174,000	$3,184
$75,000 to under $100,000	11,729,485	16,407	0.14%	$91,073,000	$5,551
$100,000 to under $200,000	13,851,341	22,957	0.17%	$155,910,000	$6,791
$200,000 and over	4,375,659	2,056	0.05%	$7,047,000	$3,428
Total	142,450,569	86,628	0.06%	$353,492,000	$3,988

Source: Table prepared by the Congressional Research Service (CRS) from Internal Revenue Service, Individual Complete Report, Publication 1304, Table 3.3.

The percentage of total tax returns using the adoption tax credit has increased since tax year 1997, the first year of the credit, when .03% of total tax returns claimed the adoption tax credit. The change to the phase-out income level made by the Economic Growth and Tax Relief Reconciliation Act (EGTRRA, P.L. 107-16)[43] significantly increased the percentage of tax returns with an adjusted gross income between $100,000 and $200,000 claiming the adoption tax credit (from .03% in tax year 2000 to .16% in tax year 2004).

Where the adoption costs are greater than the maximum value of the credit (which may be the case for some domestic private adoptions and intercountry adoptions), the taxpayer will not recover the full cost of the adoption through the adoption tax credit, even if the taxpayer can claim the maximum adoption tax credit. For example, if an adoption costs a taxpayer $30,000, the taxpayer will receive the maximum adoption tax credit if his or her AGI is between approximately $102,000 and $174,730. However, the final adoption costs will still be greater than the maximum adoption tax credit.

As a result of the phaseout (income limitation) of the tax credit, many taxpayers may not be able to take the full adoption tax credit for an adoption. This raises the policy issue of whether, and how, to expand the tax provisions to increase the use of the tax provisions, and whether federal and state subsidies may be more efficient than tax provisions in helping offset the costs of adoption.

Federal/State Subsidies Versus Tax Incentives

Congress considered the efficiency of adoption tax provisions and adoption subsidy programs in the 1980s. In 1980, the federal government began sharing (with the states) the cost of providing monthly subsidies for parents who adopt children with special needs (Adoption Assistance and Child Welfare Act of 1980, P.L. 96-272). This federal adoption assistance program, which helps parents with the ongoing costs of raising an adoptive special needs child, is authorized under Title IV-E of the Social Security Act. In 1981, the Economic Recovery Tax Act (P.L. 97-34) established an itemized tax deduction for certain costs of adopting a child with special needs. The provision was intended to encourage adoption of special needs children by relieving some of the financial burden for taxpayers.[44]

In 1986, the Tax Reform Act (P.L. 99-514) repealed the itemized deduction and instead expanded the Title IV-E program to require that states provide direct assistance to adoptive parents to help with the initial and nonrecurring costs of adopting a special needs child. That legislation also authorized federal matching grants to states for this purpose, which, as implemented, range up to $2,000 for an adoptive family, with the federal government reimbursing 50% ($1,000) of the cost to the state. In making this change, Congress believed that the itemized tax deduction provided the greatest benefit to high-income earners.[45] Congress also believed that agencies with expertise in placing children with special needs should have budgetary control over adoption assistance, and that grant programs would facilitate more appropriate federal spending than the tax system.[46]

Since 1997, however, when P.L. 104-188 first provided for an adoption tax credit, federal assistance for adoption has been provided through both grant programs and the tax code.

Special Needs Children Versus Non-special Needs Children

Although the maximum amount of qualified expenses is the same for all adoptions, a taxpayer who adopts a special needs child is assumed to have incurred the maximum amount of qualified expenses (regardless of actual expenses) and, therefore, has the maximum adoption tax credit.

Special needs children, by definition, are considered hard to place for adoption without assistance to their adoptive parents. Providing a preference for one type of adoptive child over another in the federal tax code may be viewed as unfair or inequitable—a taxpayer adopting a special needs child receives a larger tax benefit than a taxpayer adopting a non-special needs child, even if both taxpayers have the same total costs of adoption. However, the preference for special needs children is a policy decision made by Congress to encourage adoption of children who might otherwise enter adulthood without a permanent family.[47]

Domestic Adoptions Versus Intercountry Adoptions

Federal tax assistance for adoption provides incentives for both domestic (public and private) and intercountry adoptions. However, domestic adoptions are favored under the tax provisions for adoption because for a domestic adoption, qualifying expenses may be claimed even if a domestic adoption does not finalize.[48] Intercountry adoptions *must* become finalized *before* a taxpayer can claim any qualifying expenses for the tax credit or income tax exclusion.[49] Intercountry adoptions are typically considered more expensive and less predictable for finalization than domestic adoptions.[50] A family may spend a great deal of money for an intercountry adoption, but will not receive a tax benefit if something prevents the adoption from becoming final. The preference in the federal tax provisions for domestic adoption may be considered inequitable or unfair by some families that do not receive a tax benefit because their intercountry adoption was not finalized.

Expiring Provisions

A current policy issue surrounding the tax credit and income tax exclusion is the sunset of certain provisions established in the Economic Growth and Tax Relief Reconciliation Act of 2001 (EGTRRA; P.L. 107-16). EGTRRA provided for an increase in the maximum qualified expenses and increased the amount of income where the credit phaseout begins (the income limitation). However, to remain in compliance with the Congressional Budget Act, EGTRRA included a sunset provision—the changes were scheduled to expire on December 31, 2010. The Patient Protection and Affordable Care Act (P.L. 111-148) provided, *for tax years 2010 and 2011 only*, that the adoption tax credit be refundable. The Tax Relief, Unemployment Insurance Reauthorization, and Job Creation Act of 2010 (P.L. 111-312) extended the EGTRRA provisions for adoption to tax year 2012.

In 2013, prior law will take effect. Taxpayers, beginning in tax year 2013, will be allowed to claim the adoption tax for up to $6,000 in documented expenses for the adoption of special needs children only, and the income exclusion for employer provided adoption expense programs will expire. Taxpayers with incomes greater than $75,000 will receive a reduced adoption tax credit (because of the phaseout), and taxpayers with incomes greater than $115,000 ($40,000 above the threshold) will not be eligible for the adoption tax credit.

LEGISLATIVE HISTORY

As noted earlier, federal tax assistance for adoption began with the Economic Recovery Tax Act of 1981 (P.L. 97-34), which provided an itemized deduction for adoption expenses, which was repealed by the Tax

Reform Act of 1986 (P.L. 99-514). However, the 1986 law also amended Title IV-E of the Social Security Act to require states to make direct payments to parents adopting children with special needs to help offset the nonrecurring costs of adoption (attorney fees, court costs, etc.) and authorized 50% federal matching funds to states for these purposes.[51]

Several bills subsequently introduced proposed tax incentives for adoption. Tax provisions for adoption (a tax credit and income tax exclusion for employer provided adoption programs) were included in the Balanced Budget Act of 1995 (H.R. 2491, 104th Congress),[52] which was vetoed by President Clinton (for reasons unrelated to the adoption tax provisions). The Adoption Promotion and Stability Act of 1996 (H.R. 3286, 104th Congress) also proposed an adoption tax credit and income tax exclusion. The Finance Committee report on the bill noted that one justification for the adoption tax provisions was that the financial costs of adoption should not be a barrier to adoption.[53]

The Small Business and Job Protection Act of 1996 (P.L. 104-188)

P.L. 104-188 provided a federal tax credit and income tax exclusion to taxpayers for qualified adoption expenses. Qualifying expenses were limited to $5,000 for an adoption and to $6,000 for the adoption of a special needs child. P.L. 104-188 provided a phase-out provision that reduced the tax benefits for taxpayers with incomes of more than $75,000 and less than $115,000. P.L. 104-188 also included a carryover provision so that a taxpayer with more adoption tax credit than tax liability could carryover the excess tax credit for up to five years. Finally, the act provided several definitions and special rules (that remain in current law), including qualifying expenses, eligible child, child with special needs, and special rules for intercountry adoptions. P.L. 104-188 provided that beginning after December 31, 2001, only special needs adoptions would be eligible for the tax credit, and that the income tax exclusion for employer provided adoption programs would expire.

The Taxpayer Relief Act of 1997 (P.L. 105-34)

P.L. 105-34 clarified that the adoption tax credit is claimed the tax year after qualified expenses are incurred only when the adoption has not been finalized. Previously, the provision simply stated that the adoption tax credit was claimed the tax year after expenses were incurred, except for expenses incurred the tax year the adoption was finalized (which could be claimed the tax year incurred). P.L. 105-34 also conformed the definition of adjusted gross income for the phaseout of the income tax exclusion to be the same definition of adjusted gross income used for the phaseout the adoption tax credit.

IRS Restructuring and Reform Act of 1998 (P.L. 105-206)

P.L. 105-206 changed the carryover provision of the credit so that the phaseout of the credit applies only in the year in which the credit is generated and does not reduce carryover credit amounts.

The Economic Growth and Tax Relief Reconciliation Act of 2001 (EGGTRA, P.L. 107-16)

EGGTRA (P.L. 107-16) increased the limit on qualified adoption expenses to $10,000 for all children (from $5,000 for non-special needs children and $6,000 for special needs children). In addition, EGTRRA increased the income level for the beginning of the credit phaseout to $150,000 (from the previous level of $75,000) and provided an inflation adjustment for the limit on qualified adoption expenses and the phaseout income level based on the consumer price index (CPI). EGTRRA also included a sunset provision for the legislation. The changes to the adoption tax provisions were originally scheduled to expire on December 31, 2010, and as a result of subsequent legislation will expire on December 31, 2012.

Congress believed that the EGTRRA provisions were necessary to continue to encourage adoptions. This belief was based on reported increases in adoption expenses and the success of the tax credit and income tax exclusion in reducing the final costs of adoption for taxpayers.[54]

The Job Creation and Worker Assistance Act of 2002 (P.L. 107-147)

The Job Creation and Worker Assistance Act (P.L. 107-147) clarified that qualifying expenses for the adoption of children with special needs do not need to be documented. Therefore, a family seeking to adopt a child with special needs could claim the maximum credit without having to document expenses (P.L. 107-147). The conference report accompanying H.R. 1836 (EGTRRA, P.L. 107-16) provided that the maximum amount of qualifying expenses was assumed to have been claimed (without the documentation requirement) in the case of a special needs adoption for tax years beginning after 2002. However, the legislative language of EGTRRA did not make this provision clear. Therefore, a technical correction was made in P.L. 107-147.[55] P.L. 107-147 also provides that any qualifying expenses incurred prior to tax year 2002 are subject to the preEGTRRA provisions. In other words, expenses incurred prior to 2002 were limited to qualifying expenses of $5,000 for non-special needs children and $6,000 for special needs children. Taxpayers claiming expenses prior to 2002 were also subject to the phase out income level that existed prior to EGTRRA.

The Patient Protection and Affordable Care Act (P.L. 111-148)

The Patient Protection and Affordable Care Act (P.L. 111-148) provided, for *tax years 2010 and 2011 only*, that the adoption tax credit be refundable. P.L. 111-148 also increased the qualified expenses for the adoption tax credit and the income tax exclusion for employer provided adoption assistance to $13,170 for tax year 2010, with this amount indexed for inflation in 2011.

The Tax Relief, Unemployment Insurance Reauthorization, and Job Creation Act of 2010 (P.L. 111-312)

The Tax Relief, Unemployment Insurance Reauthorization, and Job Creation Act of 2010 (P.L. 111-312) extended the EGTRRA provisions for adoption to tax year 2012.

End Notes

[1] Department of Health and Human Services (HHS), Administration for Children and Families, Children's Bureau, Child Welfare Information Gateway, *How Many Children Were Adopted in 2000 and 2001?* (hereafter cited as Child Welfare Information Gateway, *How Many Children?*). To obtain these data for inclusion in the cited estimate for the total number of adoptions, the National Center for State Courts relied on various sources,

Tax Benefits for Families: Adoption 107

including direct contacts with state courts, public and private agencies, and state bureaus of vital records. The Child Welfare Information Gateway is available at http://www.childwelfare.gov/.

[2] Child Welfare Information Gateway, *How Many Children?* Adoption by a stepparent may be of any kind, but is assumed to be domestic private adoption in most cases.

[3] Department of Health and Human Services, Administration for Children and Families, Children's Bureau, Child Welfare Gateway, *Foster Care Statistics*, May 2011.

[4] Department of Health and Human Services, Administration for Children and Families, Children's Bureau, Child Welfare Gateway, *Children in Public Foster Care on September 30 of Each Year Who Are Waiting to Be Adopted, FY2002 – FY2009*, August 2010.

[5] Department of Health and Human Services, Administration for Children and Families, Children's Bureau, Child Welfare Gateway, *Foster Care Statistics,* May 2011.

[6] Evan B. Donaldson Adoption Institute, *Adoption Facts* (2006), see http://adoptioninstitute.org/research/adoptionfacts.php (hereafter referred to as The Adoption Institute: *Adoption Facts*).

[7] For more information on intercountry adoptions, see CRS Report RL30979, *Intercountry Adoption Act of 2000 and International Adoptions*, by Douglas Reid Weimer.

[8] Department of State, *Annual Report on Intercountry Adoptions, FY2010*, December 2010.

[9] Child Welfare Information Gateway, *Costs of Adopting*, February 2011.

[10] For help with the tax terms used in this report, please see CRS Report RL30110, *Federal Individual Income Tax Terms: An Explanation*, by Mark P. Keightly, or Internal Revenue Service (IRS) Publication 17, *Your Federal Income Tax*.

[11] A taxpayer can incur qualified adoption expenses throughout, and even after completing, the process to adopt a child. One example of an expense incurred at the beginning of the process is adoption fees. During the process, the taxpayer may incur travel expenses as part of the adoption process, and after completion of the adoption process, the taxpayer may incur qualified expenses for the final legal fees.

[12] In statute, the limitation is $10,000 adjusted for inflation each year beginning with tax year 2003.

[13] Department of the Treasury, *Report to the Congress on Tax Benefits for Adoption*, October 2000, pp. 2-3, and *Federal Income Tax Benefits for Adoption, Use by Taxpayers, 1999-2005*, June p. 44. The data in the report on the adoption tax credit reflect the credit taken that tax year. Taxpayers may not be able to use the full amount of the adoption tax credit in the tax year in which they incur qualified adoption expenses. They can carryover any unused adoption tax credit to future tax years (for up to five tax years).

[14] Internal Revenue Code (IRC) § 23(d)(1)(A).

[15] IRC § 23(d)(2).

[16] IRC § 23(d)(1)(B) and IRC § 23(d)(1)(C).

[17] Prior to tax year 2003, a taxpayer claiming the adoption tax credit (or using the income tax exclusion) for the adoption of a special needs child had to document the qualifying expenses.

[18] IRC § 23(d)(3)

[19] Ibid.

[20] IRC § 23(d)(2)(C).

[21] IRC § 23(e).

[22] Adjusted gross income is total taxable income after statutory adjustments. Total taxable income does not include income that is exempt from income taxes (such as veterans' benefits). Statutory adjustments reduce taxable income before exemptions and any standard

or itemized deductions. Examples of statutory adjustments are Health Savings Accounts, IRA deductions, and alimony paid. The limitation is based on adjusted gross income without regard to IRC Sections 911, 931, or 933.

[23] IRC § 23(b)(2)(A). The income limitation is $150,000 adjusted for inflation; therefore, the income limit in tax year 2010 is $182,520.

[24] Taxpayers with an income of $222,520 or more in tax year 2010.

[25] Ibid. If a married person has been living apart from his or her spouse for more than six months of the tax year, the child to be adopted has lived with the person for more than six months of the tax year, and the person has paid more than one-half of the adoption costs and the cost of the home in which the person and the child reside, the married person may claim the adoption tax credit when filing a married filing separate tax return.

[26] Ibid.

[27] Ibid.

[28] Ibid.

[29] An income tax exclusion is a form of income that is not subject to taxation. An income tax exclusion is normally not reported for tax purposes (i.e., federal income taxes and/or employment taxes). Examples of an income tax exclusion are 401(k) contributions and fringe benefits, which are not included as income for federal income taxes and/or employment taxes (Social Security and Medicare taxes) on a person's wage statement or W-2 form. They may, however, be reported separately on the form for information purposes.

[30] IRC § 137(b)(1)

[31] IRC § 137(b)(2).

[32] IRC § 137(e).

[33] IRC § 23(3)(A).

[34] IRC § 137(c), and IRS Publication 15-B, *Employer's Tax Guide to Fringe Benefits*. During the year, no more than 5% of all payments made by the adoption program can be for shareholders or owners (or their spouses or dependents). A shareholder or owner is defined as someone who owns 5% or more of the stock, capital, or profit of the business (on any day of the year).

[35] IRC §137(a)(1)

[36] *Los Angeles Times*, Business: "Personal Finance; Aid is Available to Help Ease Adoption Burden," p. C2, July 31, 2005 (hereinafter referred to as *Personal Finance; Aid is Available*).

[37] Department of Health and Human Services, Administration for Children and Families, Children's Bureau, NAIC, *Employer-Provided Adoption Benefits*, February 2011.

[38] Ibid.

[39] Ibid.

[40] Adjusted gross income is total taxable income after statutory adjustments. Total taxable income does not include income that is exempt from income taxes (such as veterans' benefits). Statutory adjustments reduce taxable income before exemptions and any standard or itemized deductions. Examples of statutory adjustments are Health Savings Accounts, IRA deductions, and alimony paid. The limitation is based on adjusted gross income without regard to IRC Sections 911, 931, or 933.

[41] IRC § 23(b)(2)(A). The income limitation is $150,000 adjusted for inflation; therefore, the income limit in tax year 2011 is $185,210.

[42] Taxpayers with an income of $225,210 or more in tax year 2010.

[43] EGTRRA (P.L. 107-16) raised the income threshold for the phaseout of the adoption tax credit from $75,000 to $150,000.

[44] Joint Committee on Taxation, *General Explanation of the Economic Recovery Tax Act of 1981*, JCS-10-87, December 29, 1981, pp. 57-58.

[45] The use of federal matching grants provided assistance to a greater range of families.

[46] Joint Committee on Taxation, *General Explanation of the Tax Reform Act of 1986*, May 4, 1987, pp. 52-53.

[47] The preference for special needs children has existed since the itemized deduction for adoption expenses, which was *only* for the adoption of a special needs child, was established by the Economic Recovery Tax Act of 1981 (P.L. 97-34). The adoption tax credit established by P.L. 104-188 also contained a preference for special needs children in the form of a higher limit on qualified expenses for the adoption of a special needs child. EGTRRA (P.L. 107-16) established that beginning in tax year 2003, a taxpayer adopting a special needs child was assumed to have the maximum amount of qualified adoption expenses for the adoption tax provisions.

[48] IRC § 23.

[49] Ibid.

[50] DHS, ACF; Children's Bureau, NAIC.

[51] Joint Committee on Taxation, *General Explanation of the Tax Reform Act of 1986*, JCS-10-87, May 4, 1987, pp. 52-53.

[52] This legislation is also referred to as the Seven-Year Balanced Budget Reconciliation Act of 1995, the original title of the legislation as passed by the House of Representatives and before the Senate amendment. The text above uses the title from the conference report (H.Rept. 104-350) agreed to by the House on November 17, 1995.

[53] U.S. Congress, Committee on Finance, S.Rept. 104-279, Adoption Promotion and Stability Act of 1995, pp. 2-5.

[54] Joint Committee on Taxation, *General Explanation of Tax Legislation in the 107th Congress*, JCS-1-03, January 24, 2003.

[55] U.S. Congress, Committee on Ways and Means, *Economic Growth and Tax Relief Reconciliation Act of 2001, Conference Report to Accompany H.R. 1836*, H.Rept. 107-84, May 26, 2001, pp. 140-141.

In: Federal Taxes and Families　　　　ISBN: 978-1-61942-864-5
Editors: T. I. Owens and R. O. Reynolds © 2012 Nova Science Publishers, Inc.

Chapter 6

FEDERAL ESTATE, GIFT AND GENERATION-SKIPPING TAXES: A DESCRIPTION OF CURRENT LAW[*]

John R. Luckey

SUMMARY

This report contains an explanation of the major provisions of the federal estate, gift, and generation-skipping transfer taxes as they apply to transfers in 2011. The discussion provides basic principles to be applied in the computation of these three transfer taxes.

The federal estate and generation-skipping taxes were resurrected by the Tax Relief, Unemployment Insurance Reauthorization, and Job Creation Act of 2010 (P.L. 111-312) after a hiatus of one year (2010). This act also provided elective options for estates of those who died in 2010.

The federal estate tax is computed through a series of adjustments and modifications of a tax base known as the "gross estate." Certain allowable deductions reduce the gross estate to the "taxable estate," to which is then added the total of all lifetime taxable gifts made by the decedent. The tax rates are applied and, after reduction for certain allowable credits, the amount of tax owed by the estate is

---

[*] This is an edited, reformatted and augmented version of a Congressional Research Service publication, CRS Report for Congress 95-416, from www.crs.gov, Prepared for Members and Committees of Congress, dated January 19, 2011.

reached. The top rate for 2011 is 35% and the exclusion amount is $5,000,000.

This discussion divides the federal gift tax into two components: the taxable gift and the gift tax computation. The federal gift tax is imposed on lifetime gifts of property. The tax depends in large part upon the fundamental element—the value of the "taxable gift." The taxable gift is determined by reducing the gross value of the gift by the available deductions and exclusions. The gift tax liability determined on the basis of the donor's taxable gifts may be reduced by the unified lifetime credit (which covers the excludible amount of $5,000,000). The annual per donee exclusion is $13,000 ($26,000 for joint gifts) for 2011. The top rate for 2011 is 35%.

The purpose of the generation-skipping transfer tax is to close a perceived loophole in the estate and gift tax system where property could be transferred to successive generations without intervening estate or gift tax consequences. There are two basic forms of generation-skipping transfers; the indirect skip, where the generation one level below the decedent receives some beneficial interest in the property before the property passes to the generation two or more levels below, and the direct skip, where the property passes directly to the generation two or more levels below the decedent. This discussion describes the tax on these types of transfers, its computation and implementation, and use of such concepts as generation assignment and inclusion ratios. The flat rate for this tax in 2011 is 35%.

INTRODUCTION

This report contains an explanation of the major provisions of the federal estate, gift, and generation-skipping transfer taxes as they apply to transfers in 2011. The enactment of the Economic Growth and Tax Relief Reconciliation Act of 2001[1] phased out the estate and generation-skipping taxes over a 10-year period, leaving the gift tax as the only federal transfer tax in 2010. The year 2010 was the first since 1916 in which there was no federal estate tax. There was also a year hiatus for the generation-skipping tax. The Tax Relief, Unemployment Insurance Reauthorization, and Job Creation Act of 2010[2] temporarily (through the end of 2012) reinstated the estate and generation-skipping taxes with lower top rates and larger exemptions and reunified the estate and gift taxes.

The federal estate and gift taxes are unified. This means that these taxes have the same rate structure. There, also, is one lifetime credit which may be applied to these taxes. For 2011 the unified credit covers an applicable amount of $5,000,000.

The federal estate, gift, and generation-skipping tax laws are rather lengthy and complex. This report discusses those major provisions which play the dominant role in the determination of estate, gift, and generation-skipping tax liability. The discussion relates only to the taxation of United States citizens and resident aliens. Different rules apply to the taxation of nonresident alien individuals.

THE FEDERAL ESTATE TAX

The federal estate tax is a tax on the estate of a decedent, levied against and paid by the estate, as opposed to an inheritance tax which is imposed on and paid by the heirs of the decedent based upon what they receive. The federal estate tax is computed through a series of adjustments and modifications of a tax base known as the "gross estate." Certain allowable deductions reduce the gross estate to the "taxable estate," to which is then added the total of all lifetime taxable gifts made by the decedent. The tax rates are then applied. The result is the decedent's estate tax which, after reduction for certain allowable credits, is the amount of tax paid by the estate. This discussion will divide the federal estate tax into three components: the gross estate, deductions from the gross estate, and computation of the tax, including allowable tax credits.

The Gross Estate: The Federal Estate Tax Base

The gross estate of a deceased individual includes both property owned by the decedent on the date of the decedent's death and certain interests in property which the decedent had transferred to another person at some time prior to the date of death. The conditions under which such property and interests in property may be included in the decedent's gross estate often constitute an important problem area in the administration of the estate tax laws.

The gross estate of a decedent includes the value of all property, real or personal, tangible or intangible, wherever situated, in which the deceased owned an interest on the date of the decedent's death.[3] The property and interests in property included in the decedent's gross estate are valued at their fair market value on the date of death or, if elected by the executor, the alternate valuation date. The alternate valuation date is the earlier of the date of distribution or disposition of the property by the estate or the date six months after the date of death.[4] The "fair market value" of property is normally described as the price at which a willing buyer would purchase the property and a willing seller would sell it, both being fully informed as to all relevant facts. It is, consequently, the value of the property at its "highest and best use," rather than its current use.[5] There is, however, a special rule under which the real estate used in certain family farms and closely held businesses will, under certain conditions, be valued for estate tax purposes at less than its highest and best use.[6]

Certain types of property are included in a decedent's gross estate under special rules. The proceeds from a life insurance policy on the life of the deceased will be included in the decedent's gross estate if either the proceeds are payable to or for the use of the executor or the estate, or if the decedent held any "incidents of ownership" in the policy on the date of death or gave away such incidents of ownership within three years of the date of death.[7] An incident of ownership is an economic right in the policy, such as the right to cancel the policy, change the beneficiary, or borrow against its cash surrender value. The value of a survivor's annuity payable because of the death of the decedent will be included in the decedent's gross estate if the deceased had the right to receive a lifetime annuity under the same contract.[8]

The value of property owned by the decedent jointly with a right of survivorship in another person, other than the decedent's spouse, is fully included in the decedent's gross estate, except to the extent it can be shown that someone other than the decedent contributed money or money's worth of consideration towards the cost of acquiring the property.[9] Only one-half of the value of property owned jointly with a right of survivorship by a decedent and the surviving spouse will be included in the decedent's gross estate, regardless of the relative contributions of the decedent and the surviving spouse.[10]

In a number of instances, the value of a decedent's gross estate includes the value of property not owned by the decedent on the date of death. A decedent's gross estate includes the value of lifetime gifts over which the decedent retained a life interest[11] or a power to alter, amend, terminate, or destroy the beneficial enjoyment of the property.[12] The value of lifetime gifts which are not to take effect until the date of death are also included in the donor's gross estate.[13] The gross estate includes the value of these types of property which have been transferred, irrespective of the number of years which have elapsed between the date of the gift and the date of the donor's death. The value of property sold during the decedent's lifetime, for full and adequate consideration in money or money's worth, is not included in the decedent's gross estate under these sections of the Internal Revenue Code.

The gross estate also includes the value of interests in property given away within three years of the date of death if, had the property been retained, it would have been included in the decedent's gross estate under one of the three special rules noted above or under special rules for life insurance proceeds. Property given away within three years of the date of death is also included in the decedent's gross estate for purposes of qualifying for certain estate and income tax benefits.[14]

The value of all property subject to a general power of appointment held by the decedent on the date of death will be included in the decedent's gross estate, even if the decedent died without exercising the power. A power of appointment is a right, held by a person other than the owner of property, to determine who will enjoy the ownership of or benefit of the property. A power of appointment is "general" if it may be exercised by its holder in favor of the holder, the holder's estate, the holder's creditors, or the creditors of the holder's estate. If a power cannot be exercised in favor of these classes of persons, it is not a general power of appointment, regardless of the size of the classes of beneficiaries in whose favor the power can be exercised.[15]

Deductions from the Gross Estate: Reaching the Taxable Estate

A decedent's taxable estate is determined by reducing the gross estate by allowable deductions, including estate administration expenses, certain debts and losses, the amount of qualified transfers to a surviving spouse, charitable bequests, and State death taxes.

The first deduction to which an estate is entitled is for the funeral expenses, administration expenses, claims against the estate, and unpaid mortgages paid by the estate (to the extent not reflected in the reduced value of estate assets). These payments may be deducted to the extent that they are paid by the estate and to the extent they are allowable under the laws of the applicable jurisdiction in which the estate is administered.[16] Additionally, the estate may deduct the amount of any casualty or theft losses sustained by the estate during settlement, to the extent such losses are not compensated by insurance.[17]

The estate is also entitled to a "marital deduction" for the value of all property passing to the decedent's surviving spouse.[18] Interests which may terminate in favor of another person upon the lapse of time, the occurrence of an event or contingency, or the failure of an event or contingency to occur, generally do not qualify for the estate tax marital deduction.[19] The estate tax marital deduction is allowed only for non-terminable interests passing to the surviving spouse. These interests may pass to the spouse under the terms of the decedent's will, by law of intestacy, by contract, by operation of law, or otherwise. Special exceptions to the terminable interest rule are made for certain transfers in trust of a lifetime income interest if the executor elects to include the value of the trust property in the surviving spouse's gross estate, and for certain life estates coupled with a general power of appointment, as well as for certain life insurance settlement options and certain interests conditioned upon survivorship for a reasonable period not exceeding six months.[20]

The gross estate is also reduced by the value of certain charitable bequests and devises to qualified charitable organizations.[21] An estate tax deduction is generally permitted for any transfer which, if made during the decedent's lifetime would have been deductible for income tax purposes, though the rules are not identical.[22]

The gross estate is also reduced by the amount of any estate, inheritance, legacy, or succession taxes actually paid to any State or the District of Columbia in respect to property included in the gross estate.[23]

Computation of the Estate Tax Liability

Under the unified estate and gift tax system, computation of a decedent's estate tax liability requires a grossed-up, a combining, of the decedent's lifetime taxable gifts and the decedent's taxable estate to which the tax rate schedule is applied. Then, any available credits are taken to obtain the decedent's actual estate tax liability.[24]

The estate rate schedule[25] is as follows:

Taxable Estate	Tentative Tax
not over $10,000	18% of such amount
$10,000-$20,000	$1,800 + 20% of excess over $10,000
$20,000-$40,000	$3,800 + 22% of excess over $20,000
$40,000-$60,000	$8,200 + 24% of excess over $40,000
$60,000-$80,000	$13,000 + 26% of excess over $60,000

Taxable Estate	Tentative Tax
$80,000-$100,000	$18,200 + 28% of excess over $80,000
$100,000-$150,000	$23,800 + 30% of excess over $100,000
$150,000-$250,000	$38,800 + 32% of excess over $150,000
$250,000-$500,000	$70,800 + 34% of excess over $250,000
$500,000 +	35% of excess over $500,000

There are three major estate tax credits presently in effect: the unified transfer tax credit, the credit for foreign death taxes, and the credit for federal estate taxes paid by previous estates. Each credit is a dollar-for-dollar offset against an estate's federal estate tax liability.

The unified tax credit is available against both lifetime gift tax liabilities and the estate tax liability. To the extent this credit is used to offset gift taxes, it is unavailable to offset estate taxes. The credit is expressed in the code as an "applicable exclusion amount," that is, the amount of taxable gifts or estate that the credit would cover. The applicable exclusion amount in 2011 is $5,000,000.[26] A surviving spouse may also use any unused applicable exclusion amount of their spouse.[27]

Each estate is also allowed credits for foreign death taxes, including estate, inheritance, legacy, or succession taxes actually paid by the estate or any heir with respect to property included in the federal gross estate. This credit is limited to the amount of U.S. estate taxes paid on the same property. The credit is computed as the same proportionate share of the total U.S. estate taxes as the value of the foreign taxed property bears to the total of the U.S. taxable estate.[28]

The credit for previously taxed property (the PTP credit) is provided to relieve some of the harshness that could otherwise result when an individual dies soon after inheriting property upon which a federal estate tax has already been imposed. The PTP credit is allowed for all or some portion of the federal estate taxes paid on property transferred to the decedent within the past ten years. The PTP credit is graduated according to the amount of time that has elapsed between the date the property was transferred to the decedent and the date of death.

The maximum PTP credit is 100% of the previously paid taxes, when the decedent received the property within the first two years prior to the date of death. The minimum PTP credit is 20% of the previously paid taxes, when the decedent received the property during the ninth or tenth years preceding the date of death.[29]

The Federal Gift Tax

The federal gift tax is imposed on lifetime gifts of property.[30] The tax depends in large part upon the fundamental element—the value of the "taxable gift." The taxable gift is determined by reducing the gross value of the gift by the available deductions and exclusions. The gift tax liability determined on the basis of the donor's taxable gifts may be reduced by the available unified transfer tax credit.

The Taxable Gift

Determining the amount of a taxable gift is fundamental to determining the donor's ultimate gift tax liability. The amount of the taxable gift is the fair market value of the gift at the time it was made, less certain exclusions and deductions.[31] The major deductions and exclusions are the annual per donee exclusion, the gift tax marital deduction, and the gift tax charitable deduction.

Every donor may exclude from the federal gift tax base the first $13,000 of cash or property given to each donee annually.[32] An unlimited exclusion is available for gifts made by paying an individual's tuition or medical expenses. The annual exclusion is unavailable, however, for gifts of future interests which vest in the donee only upon some future date. The present interest rule often requires complicated drafting techniques to obtain the annual exclusion for the value of a gift of a life insurance policy made in trust, or a gift to a minor, to be held in trust until the minor reaches a certain age.[33]

Married couples may double the annual exclusion through "gift-splitting," an arrangement in which one spouse consents to being treated as having made one-half of the gifts made by his or her spouse in that taxable year.[34] The election is made by a notation on the gift tax return, and results in each spouse receiving a $13,000 per donee exclusion for one-half of the value of the same gift. Therefore, married couples may annually exclude $26,000 per donee from tax by gift-splitting.

A deduction is also allowed for all of the value of certain interspousal gifts.[35] Like its estate tax counterpart, no gift tax marital deduction is allowed for most gifts of terminable interests.[36]

A donor may also deduct the value of certain charitable gifts. The value of the gift may be deducted only if the charity is of a type described in the applicable statutory provision, which describes most, but not all, of the charities for which deductible income tax contributions may be made.[37]

The division of property incident to a divorce or separation agreement may result in the interspousal transfer of property for a consideration which is not adequate for gift tax purposes. Consequently, the Code provides that interspousal transfers pursuant to a written agreement dividing the property of the spouses and occurring within two years before and one year after a decree of divorce will not be treated as taxable gifts, as long as the marital rights of the spouses are settled by the agreement or it provides for a reasonable allowance for the support of minor children.[38]

The renunciation of property given one by another person might be viewed as either the negation of the initial gift, resulting in no gift tax liability, or as a reciprocal gift, resulting in two gift tax liabilities. If a disclaimer is made in writing, before the donee has accepted any benefits of the property, and within nine months of the date the gift was made, the gift will be ignored for gift tax purposes.[39]

The Gift Tax Computation

The tax on a taxable gift is measured initially by the value of the transferred property, and is cumulative in nature.[40] The applicable rate of tax on a taxable gift is determined by the total of the donor's lifetime taxable gifts The estate and gift tax rate tables are identical.[41]

The actual computation of the gift tax for each calendar year is completed in three steps. First, the donor's taxable gifts for the calendar year and any preceding calendar periods are totaled and the tentative tax determined. Second, the tentative tax is calculated on the total taxable gifts for preceding calendar periods. Third, the result from step two is subtracted from the result of step one, and the donor's unused unified tax credit is applied to the remaining amount.[42]

THE TAX ON GENERATION-SKIPPING TRANSFERS

The Tax Reform Act of 1986 repealed the generation-skipping transfer tax, enacted in 1976, as being unduly complicated and replaced it with a simplified flat-rate tax.[43] The purpose of the resulting generation-skipping transfer tax is the same as predecessor, to close a loophole in the estate and gift tax system where property could be transferred to successive generations without paying multiple estate or gift taxes. The traditional generation-skipping transfers were trusts established by a parent for the life time benefit of the children with the remainder passing to the grandchildren. If properly drafted, no estate or gift tax would be imposed when the trust corpus passed from the settlor's children to the settlor's grandchildren because the estate tax is not imposed on interests which terminate at death.

There are two basic forms of generation-skipping transfers; the indirect skip, where the generation one level below the decedent (e.g., children) receives some beneficial interest in the property before the property passes to the generation two or more levels below (e.g., grandchildren), and the direct skip, where the property passes directly to the generation two or more levels below the decedent (e.g., grandchildren). The 1976 law only taxed the indirect skip. The current system taxes both types of transfers.

The generation-skipping tax is a flat-rate tax. The rate is set at the highest estate tax rate, currently 35%.[44] This tax rate is applied to three different events, a taxable distribution, a taxable termination, or a direct skip.

A taxable distribution is a distribution from a trust, other than a taxable termination or direct skip, to a skip person.[45] A skip person is a person assigned to a generation two or more generations below the transferor's.[46]

A taxable termination is a termination by death, lapse of time, release of power, or otherwise of an interest in property held in trust, unless immediately after the termination a non-skip person has an interest in the property or at no time after the termination may a distribution be made from the trust to a skip person.[47]

A direct skip is a transfer to a skip person. A transfer to a trust is a direct skip if all the interests in the trust are held by skip persons.[48]

All persons are assigned a generation level under the statute. Persons related to the transferor or spouse are assigned along family lines. For example, the transferor, spouse, and brothers and sisters are in one generation, their children in the next and grandchildren the next. Lineal descendants of a grandparent of the transferor or spouse are assigned to generations on the same basis. Anyone ever married to a lineal descendant of the transferor's grandparent or the spouse's grandparent are assigned to the level of their spouse who was a lineal descendant. Non-relatives of the transferor are assigned generations measured from the birth of the transferor. Persons not more than 12 1/2 years younger are treated as members of the same generation as the transferor. Each 25-year period thereafter is treated as a new generation. A grandchild of the transferor or spouse is moved up one generation if his parents are deceased at the time of the transfer.[49]

Several exemptions or exclusions are provided in the statutory scheme.[50] The exclusions for tuition and medical expense payments from the gift tax[51] also apply to the generation-skipping tax.[52] The $13,000 per donee annual exclusion from the gift tax is recognized against taxation of direct skips only (i.e., where the property passes directly to the generation two or more levels below the decedent).[53] A $5,000,000 GST exemption is allowed to each individual for generation-skipping transfers during life or at death.[54] Again, the exemption is doubled for married individuals who elect to treat the transfers as made one-half by each.[55]

The GST exemption may be allocated by the transferor or the executor to any generation-skipping transfer. Once the allocation is made it is irrevocable. Unless a contrary election is made, all or any portion of the exclusion not previously allocated is deemed allocated to a lifetime direct skip to the extent necessary to make the inclusion ratio for the transfer zero.[56]

The inclusion ratio is figured by subtracting from one a fraction, the numerator of which is the portion of the GST exemption allocated to the transfer, the denominator of which is the value of the property transferred.[57] To compute the generation-skipping tax, the value of the transfer is multiplied by the tax rate (35%) and by the inclusion ratio.[58]

The liability for the tax is determined by the type of transfer. In the case of a taxable distribution, the tax is paid by the transferee. The tax on taxable terminations or direct skips from a trust is paid by the trustee. Direct skips, other than those from a trust, are taxed to the transferor.[59]

ELECTIONS AVAILABLE TO ESTATES OF INDIVIDUALS WHO DIED IN 2010

The year 2010 was the first since 1916 in which there was no federal estate tax, but heirs of decedents who died in 2010 were subject to carry-over basis in inherited property. There was also a year hiatus for the generation-skipping tax. The Tax Relief, Unemployment Insurance Reauthorization, and Job Creation Act of 2010[60] temporarily (through the end of 2012) reinstated the estate and generation-skipping taxes with lower top rates and larger exemptions, reunified the estate and gift taxes, and reinstituted stepped-up basis rules (discussed below) for property received from a decedent. The act provided for an election for 2010 estates to either use the carryover basis rules which were in effect in 2010 or opt to have the reinstated estate tax regimen apply to the estate, with the benefit of the stepped-up basis rules. Which option is more beneficial depends on the size of the estate, whether the assets are to be sold, and the nature and basis of the property in the estate.

Technically, basis rules are income tax rules, not estate tax rules. Basis is used to determine gain on the sale of capital assets for income tax purposes. Often basis and cost are equivalent. Generally, to determine taxable income from sale of a capital asset, the basis in that asset is subtracted from the sale price. Prior to 2010 and currently the basis in property received from a decedent was/is a "stepped-up" basis.[61] The inheritor of property, instead of having the basis of the one from whom he received the property (a carry-over basis), has a basis in the property of its fair market value at the date of death of the decedent. The purpose of the stepped-up basis rule is to avoid double taxation. The property has been subject to the estate tax. If the property had a carry-over basis and was sold after inheritance, there would be a capital gain subject to the income tax. The use of the stepped-up basis eliminates this capital gain and thus the income tax on the sale.

In 2010 there was no federal estate tax. Therefore, there was no chance of this type of double taxation and thus this need for the stepped-up basis rules was removed. In 2010 the basis in property received from a decedent was the lesser of carry-over basis or the fair market value of the property on the date of death of the decedent.[62] Under the estate tax and the income tax stepped-up basis rules, an amount of the gross estate was not subject to either tax.[63] To avoid penalizing decedents with estates below the estate tax threshold (whose property would have otherwise received a carry-over basis), two amounts of property received from a decedent still received stepped-up basis. Every estate could allocate $1,300,000 basis increase to property in the estate.[64] In addition to this general step-up, property which passed to the spouse of the decedent could be allocated up to $3,000,000 basis increase.[65]

End Notes

[1] P.L. 107-16, 107th Cong., 1st Sess. (2001).

[2] P.L. 111-312, 111th Cong. 2nd Sess. (2010).

[3] 26 U.S.C. § 2031(a).

[4] 26 U.S.C. § 2032(a). The alternate valuation date is useful when the value of the property contained in the gross estate has decreased following the death of the decedent, such as might be the case when the estate holds a substantial quantity of stock in a corporation in which the decedent was a dominant figure.

[5] Treas. Regs. (26 C.F.R.) § 20.2031-1(b).

[6] 26 U.S.C. § 2032A. An election for special use valuation may be made by the executor where the majority of the estate is made up of closely-held business property. Under this election the executor may choose to value the property at its closely-held business value rather than its value at its highest and best use. The special use valuation cannot, however, reduce the gross estate by more than $1,020,000 in 2011 (This limit is indexed for inflation each year).

[7] 26 U.S.C. § 2042.

[8] 26 U.S.C. § 2039(a). Annuities are valued according to the actuarial life expectancy of the annuitant, the frequency of the payments, and the size of the payments. Treas. Regs. Sec. 20.2039-1.

[9] 26 U.S.C. § 2040(a).

[10] 26 U.S.C. 2040(b).

[11] 26 U.S.C. § 2036. The retention of an estate, the duration of which is not ascertainable except with reference to the lifetime of the donor, is also treated as a retained life interest, as is the retention of the right to vote the stock of certain closely-held corporations. 26 U.S.C. § 2036(b); *see also, United States v. Byrum*, 408 U.S. 125 (1972).

[12] 26 U.S.C. § 2038. These transfers are also known as "revocable transfers" because the retained power allowed the deceased donor to revoke the transfer and return to himself or herself the enjoyment of the transferred property.

[13] 26 U.S.C. § 2037.

[14] 26 U.S.C. § 2035.

[15] 26 U.S.C. § 2041. Certain other powers are statutorily classified as limited or non-special powers of appointment, including the right to invade the corpus (principal) subject to the power, only under an ascertainable standard relating to health, education, support or maintenance, or the non-cumulative right to withdraw up to the greater of $5,000 or 5% of corpus annually.

[16] 26 U.S.C. § 2053.

[17] 26 U.S.C. § 2054.

[18] 26 U.S.C. § 2056.

[19] 26 U.S.C. § 2056(b). Generally, the unlimited marital deduction is not allowed for transfers to a surviving spouse who is not a citizen of the United States and does not become a citizen before the estate tax return is filed unless the transfer utilizes a qualified domestic trust. See 26 U.S.C. § 2056(d). A qualified domestic trust is defined in 26 U.S.C. § 2056A to be a trust which has at least one trustee who is a United States citizen and which citizen trustee has veto power over distributions from the trust.

[20] 26 U.S.C. § 2056(b).

[21] 26 U.S.C. § 2055.

[22] *Compare*, 26 U.S.C. §§ 2055(a) and 170(c).

[23] 26 U.S.C. § 2058.

[24] 26 U.S.C. § 2001(b).

[25] 26 U.S.C. § 2001(c). Because of the applicable exclusion amount of $5,000,000, estates which actually pay the federal estate tax have basically a flat rate of 35%.

[26] 26 U.S.C. § 2010.

[27] 26 U.S.C. § 2010(c).

[28] 26 U.S.C. § 2014.

[29] 26 U.S.C. § 2013.

[30] The word "gift" is not defined in the tax laws, but the Code does state that the amount of a gift is ascertained when "property is transferred for less than an adequate and full consideration in money or money's worth," 26 U.S.C. § 2512(b). Generally, the regulations state that a

gift is made, for gift tax purposes, when there is a transfer for inadequate consideration and the transaction does not take place in a business context. Treas. Regs. § 25.2511. This should be distinguished from the definition of a "gift" for income tax purposes, which requires that the transfer be made from "detached and disinterested generosity." *Comm'r v. Duberstein*, 363 U.S. 278 (1960). A transfer may, therefore, be a gift for gift tax purposes, because there was no legally sufficient consideration, but not constitute a gift for income tax purposes, because it was not motivated by detached and disinterested generosity.

[31] 26 U.S.C. § 2512. Special valuation rules for valuation freezing transactions are set forth in 26 U.S.C. § 2701 through 2704.

[32] 26 U.S.C. § 2503. This figure is indexed for inflation.

[33] But see 26 U.S.C. § 2503(c), for a special rule granting the annual exclusion for gifts to certain trusts created for the benefit of minors which permit the income to be expended for the benefit of the minor until the minor attains age 21, and requires the minor to be given outright ownership of the trust assets at that age or, if the minor should die prior to attaining age 21, to designate by will or otherwise the disposition of the property.

[34] 26 U.S.C. § 2513. Gift-splitting also permits use of both spouses' unified transfer tax credits to eliminate present tax on lifetime taxable gifts.

[35] 26 U.S.C. § 2523(a).

[36] 26 U.S.C. § 2523(b),(f).

[37] 26 U.S.C. § 2522, *compare*, 26 U.S.C. § 170(c).

[38] 26 U.S.C. § 2516.

[39] 26 U.S.C. § 2518.

[40] 26 U.S.C. § 2501.

[41] 26 U.S.C. § 2001(c).

[42] 26 U.S.C. §§ 2502, 2001(c), 2505. P.L. 111-312 restored the total unification of the unified credit so that the full applicable exclusion amount is available to offset gifts. The 35% top rate must be used for computing the amount of credit used when grossing up any previously made gifts where a higher rate was used.

[43] Staff of the Joint Committee on Taxation, 100th Cong., 1st Sess., *General Explanation of the Tax Reform Act of 1986*, 1263 (1987). P.L. 11-312 brought back the generation-skipping transfer tax after a hiatus for 2010.

[44] 26 U.S.C. § 2641(a).

[45] 26 U.S.C. § 2612.

[46] 26 U.S.C. § 2613.

[47] 26 U.S.C. § 2612.

[48] 26 U.S.C. § 2612.

[49] 26 U.S.C. § 2651.

[50] P.L. 99-514, § 1433(b)(3) provided that for transfers made prior to January 1, 1990, each grantor could exempt $2,000,000 in direct skips per grandchild ($4,000,000 for married individuals who elect to treat the transfers as made one-half by each).

[51] 26 U.S.C. § 2503.

[52] 26 U.S.C. § 2611(b).

[53] 26 U.S.C. § 2642(c).

[54] 26 U.S.C. § 2631. The GST exemption is to be equal to the estate tax applicable exclusion amount.

[55] 26 U.S.C. § 2652.

[56] 26 U.S.C. § 2632.

[57] 26 U.S.C. § 2642.

[58] 26 U.S.C. § 2641.
[59] 26 U.S.C. § 2603.
[60] P.L. 111-312, 111th Cong. 2nd Sess. (2010).
[61] 26 U.S.C. § 1014.
[62] P.L. 107-16, § 542.
[63] The applicable exclusion amount and all property passing to the spouse under the unlimited marital deduction would not be subject to the estate tax while still receiving the stepped-up basis and thus avoiding the income tax on the subsequent sale of the property.
[64] P.L. 107-16, § 542. A decedent who is a nonresident and not a citizen is limited to a $60,000 step-up.
[65] P.L. 107-16, § 542.

INDEX

A

Administration for Children and Families, 106, 107, 108
adults, 16, 17, 18, 19, 20
Afghanistan, 48
age, vii, 4, 12, 17, 20, 40, 41, 44, 45, 46, 70, 75, 77, 80, 81, 84, 86, 95, 96, 118, 124
agencies, 93, 102, 107
alternative minimum tax (AMT), vii, 3, 11, 39, 46, 50, 55
American Recovery and Reinvestment Act, viii, 2, 3, 31, 36, 41, 48, 53, 54, 64
American Samoa, 50, 72, 74
assets, 16, 74, 115, 122, 124

B

base, 11, 12, 19, 23, 111, 113, 118
beneficiaries, 16, 115
bonuses, 2, 3, 4, 15, 24, 25, 28, 29
Bureau of Labor Statistics, 74

C

capital gains, 11, 56, 59, 74
caregivers, viii, 78, 79, 82, 85, 87
cash, viii, 23, 24, 36, 56, 57, 58, 59, 62, 68, 72, 114, 118
Census, 28, 29, 33, 74
charitable organizations, 116, 118
Chicago, 32
child tax credit, viii, 35, 36, 37, 38, 39, 40, 41, 43, 44, 45, 46, 47, 48, 49, 50, 51, 53, 54, 55, 56, 57, 58, 59, 60, 61, 62, 63, 64, 65, 66, 67, 68, 69, 70, 71, 72, 73, 74
complexity, 57, 61, 70, 71
computation, 111, 112, 113, 116, 119
Conference Report, 51, 109
Congress, vii, viii, 1, 3, 31, 35, 36, 41, 44, 45, 47, 48, 49, 50, 51, 53, 54, 59, 60, 61, 62, 65, 70, 72, 73, 77, 78, 85, 91, 101, 102, 104, 105, 107, 109, 111
consumer price index, 67, 105
consumption, 12, 16, 17, 32
cost, 16, 17, 23, 24, 31, 32, 43, 45, 48, 54, 61, 62, 65, 66, 69, 72, 79, 80, 86, 88, 101, 102, 108, 114, 122

D

deduction, 5, 6, 7, 8, 9, 11, 14, 19, 26, 27, 31, 44, 59, 69, 71, 72, 86, 87, 101, 103, 109, 115, 116, 118, 123, 125
Department of Agriculture, 73
Department of Health and Human Services, 93, 99, 106, 107, 108
Department of the Treasury, 74, 107

dependent care assistance programs (DCAP), viii, 78
dependent care tax credit (DCTC), viii, 77, 78
direct payment, 47, 83, 99, 104
distribution, 1, 13, 19, 32, 63, 72, 114, 120, 121
District of Columbia, 86, 116

E

earned income credit (EIC), vii, 2
earnings, 3, 10, 13, 15, 28, 32, 35, 37, 38, 39, 40, 48, 49, 50, 53, 55, 57, 58, 60, 62, 65, 66, 67, 68, 71, 72, 73, 74
economics, 16, 61
education, 16, 75, 80, 89, 123
, 41, 42, 48
Emergency Economic Stabilization Act (EESA), 41, 42, 48
employees, 84, 89, 99
employers, 84, 99
employment, 39, 77, 79, 80, 81, 84, 85, 108
equity, 1, 2, 3, 12, 13, 14, 15, 18, 19, 24, 25, 30, 54, 55, 57, 58, 59, 60, 61, 73
exclusion, viii, ix, 11, 21, 24, 32, 48, 77, 78, 79, 84, 91, 92, 94, 98, 99, 103, 104, 105, 106, 107, 108, 112, 117, 118, 121, 123, 124, 125
expenditures, 74

F

fairness, 13, 15, 54, 55, 57, 58
family characteristics, 12, 16
family income, 17
family members, 7, 17, 19, 21, 22
farms, 114
federal assistance, 91, 92, 102
financial, viii, 36, 44, 48, 54, 60, 70, 101, 104
formula, 32, 35, 37, 38, 39, 40, 41, 43, 46, 47, 49, 50, 51, 55, 60, 62, 66, 72, 73, 85

G

GDP deflator, 6, 31
goods and services, 12
grant programs, 91, 102
grants, vii, ix, 91, 92, 102, 109

H

Health and Human Services (HHS), 93, 99, 106, 107, 108
history, vii, 15, 32, 35, 36, 55, 72, 92
horizontal equity, 13, 15, 18, 24, 30, 57, 58, 59, 73
House of Representatives, 109
household tasks, 23
human resources, 32

I

imitation, 97, 101, 108
imputed income, 12, 23, 24, 32
income tax treatment, vii, 2
incompatibility, 15
indexing, 11, 67, 69
individuals, 1, 4, 8, 9, 10, 11, 12, 14, 15, 16, 20, 25, 28, 29, 30, 31, 77, 80, 84, 87, 93, 95, 113, 121, 124
inflation, 4, 5, 6, 10, 31, 37, 39, 44, 45, 46, 47, 51, 53, 55, 66, 67, 69, 73, 74, 86, 91, 92, 95, 105, 106, 107, 108, 123, 124
inheritance, 113, 116, 117, 122
Internal Revenue Service (IRS), 14, 31, 32, 38, 74, 79, 89, 95, 96, 100, 107
investment, 16, 17, 56, 59
Iraq, 48
IRC, 50, 95, 107, 108, 109
itemized deductions, 1, 6, 8, 9, 12, 21, 24, 28, 31, 108

J

jurisdiction, 115

justification, 17, 104

L

labor force participation, 9
laws, vii, 4, 8, 36, 41, 62, 80, 113, 115, 123
legislation, 5, 9, 15, 31, 41, 44, 45, 49, 64, 102, 105, 109
life expectancy, 123
lifetime, 111, 112, 113, 114, 116, 117, 118, 119, 121, 123, 124
Louisiana, 86
lower-income families, vii, 2, 3, 10, 14, 18, 31, 53, 61, 65, 66, 69

M

marital status, 28, 98
marriage, vii, 2, 3, 4, 5, 6, 7, 8, 9, 10, 11, 12, 15, 24, 25, 27, 28, 29, 30, 31, 74
married couples, 1, 2, 5, 8, 10, 11, 12, 15, 20, 23, 24, 25, 28, 30, 31, 35, 69, 118
median, 86
Medicaid, 70
medical, 12, 96, 118, 121
Medicare, 84, 99, 108
middle class, vii, viii, 3, 36, 49
military, 48
modifications, 54, 62, 63, 64, 66, 73, 111, 113

N

National Survey, 89
nursing home, 80

O

Obama, vii, ix, 3, 78, 85, 87, 88, 89
Office of Management and Budget, 65, 74
ownership, 114, 115, 124

P

parents, viii, ix, 11, 12, 15, 16, 17, 28, 29, 30, 35, 39, 50, 63, 72, 77, 78, 83, 86, 92, 96, 101, 102, 104, 120
payroll, 3, 5, 12, 13, 39, 40, 46, 50, 59, 69, 72, 84, 89
penalties, 2, 3, 15, 24, 25, 28, 29, 30
policy issues, 92, 99
policy makers, 54, 61, 66 71
policy options, viii, 49, 53, 54, 55
poverty, 4, 14, 18, 20
President Clinton, 45, 104
President Obama, vii, ix, 3, 78, 85, 87
principles, 15, 16, 44, 111
progressive tax, 14, 17, 30, 32, 58
progressive tax system, 14, 17, 58
Puerto Rico, 50, 72, 74
purchasing power, 4, 5

R

real estate, 114
reform, vii, 3, 6, 14, 18, 31, 70, 74, 75, 101, 104, 105, 109, 119, 124
regulations, 79, 80, 123
relief, 4, 10, 16, 17, 29, 41, 44, 69, 74
Republican Party, 44
requirements, 40, 41, 73, 98
rules, 3, 30, 46, 70, 71, 82, 84, 94, 98, 99, 104, 113, 114, 115, 116, 121, 122, 124

S

Samoa, 50, 72, 74
savings, 23, 32, 56, 59, 89
Senate, 45, 48, 51, 109
services, 12, 16, 23, 32, 48, 79, 80, 88
Social Security, 10, 12, 13, 41, 50, 51, 56, 59, 84, 89, 96, 98, 99, 101, 104, 108
spending, 16, 65, 70, 89, 102
SSI, 56, 59
standard of living, 16, 18, 20, 24

state, vii, ix, 8, 15, 57, 79, 80, 91, 92, 93, 94, 95, 96, 101, 102, 104, 107, 123
stock, 122, 123
structure, vii, viii, 4, 7, 8, 9, 12, 13, 15, 17, 22, 24, 25, 27, 35, 36, 50, 54, 55, 56, 57, 58, 59, 60, 62, 112
subsidy, 8, 10, 20, 60, 73, 101
succession, 116, 117

T

Task Force, ix, 78
tax base, 111, 113, 118
tax credits, 13, 15, 37, 51, 57, 67, 74, 117, 124
tax cuts, vii, 1, 3, 14
tax deduction, 44, 101, 102, 116
tax incentive, viii, 78, 91, 104
tax policy, 15, 17
tax rates, vii, 1, 3, 7, 9, 13, 18, 19, 20, 21, 23, 24, 25, 30, 31, 32, 51, 58, 59, 72, 74, 84, 111, 113
tax system, 13, 14, 15, 16, 17, 19, 20, 23, 32, 50, 58, 60, 69, 72, 92, 102, 112, 116, 119
tax threshold, 122
taxation, 7, 15, 16, 17, 22, 32, 48, 108, 113, 121, 122
Taxpayer Relief Act, viii, 5, 36, 41, 44, 45, 46, 50, 54, 104
Title I, 96, 101, 104

Title IV, 96, 101, 104
transfer payments, 56, 59, 70
Treasury, 29, 45, 47, 51, 74, 89, 107
treatment, vii, 1, 2, 3, 7, 8, 9, 14, 15, 17, 18, 22, 23, 24, 25, 30, 31, 78, 93

U

U.S. Department of Agriculture, 73
U.S. Department of the Treasury, 89
uniform, 23, 71, 75, 80
United States, 74, 94, 96, 113, 123
Urban Institute, 74, 89

V

valuation, 114, 122, 123, 124
vertical equity, 13, 19, 57, 58
Vice President, ix, 78, 85

W

wages, 56, 59, 89
Washington, 32, 33, 50
welfare, 10, 12, 19, 93, 96
well-being, 17, 80
White House, ix, 78
workers, viii, 61, 73, 78, 89
workforce, viii, 77, 78